Janet Reed Aug 10/ 1995
From Jackie

1504
Published in the USA 1995 by JG Press
Distributed by World Publications, Inc
Copyright © 1994 by Colour Library Books Ltd, Godalming, Sur
All rights reserved
No part of this book may be reproduced or transmitted in any
form or by any means, electronic or mechanical, including
photocopying, recording, or by any information storage and
retrieval system, without permission in writing from the Publishe
Printed and Bound in Singapore
ISBN 1-57215-016-5

The JG Press imprint is a trademark of JG Press, Inc.
455 Somerset Avenue
North Dighton, MA 02764

# WOK COOKING

# Contents

# Introduction

The wok is an ancient Chinese cooking utensil known for its versatility. It can be used for stir-frying, deep frying, steaming, boiling and braising a wide variety of food.

Stir-Fried Leeks and Lamb (above), Beef and Oyster Sauce (above right) and Pork with Plum Sauce (right).

The traditional wok is made of heavy gauge carbon steel which conducts heat well, giving a quick high temperature. However, this medium will rust if not oiled and given proper care. Lengthy cooking in liquid may impart a metallic taste to the food or may cause the discolouration of white liquids or food. Aluminum and stainless steel woks are also available and are a good choice, particularly if steaming, braising, boiling, or cooking for a long time. These woks need no seasoning but do not heat as efficiently as carbon steel.

Cooking times in this book are only a guide, as actual times will vary with the kind of wok you use and the intensity of the heat source. There are three types of wok: round-bottomed, for use on gas burners – with the use of a ring-base for stability; flat bottomed, for electric ranges; and electric woks, which can be used to cook at the table or anywhere there is an outlet. Other equipment that may be needed includes a curved, long-handled spatula, and curved slotted spoon (which fit into the curved shape of the wok), a domed lid, a metal trivet or bamboo steamer and a deep fat frying thermometer.

**Stir-frying,** a fuel and timesaver. It is unique to wok cooking, where small pieces of food are toss-cooked in minutes over intense heat, in a very small amount of oil. The shape of the wok allows for tossing with abandon. Food is cooked in a matter of minutes and the flavors and juices are sealed in, resulting in succulent meat, poultry and seafood, and tender and crisp vegetables. Nutritional values are retained, as are the fresh and bright colors of vegetables.

A number of steps followed will lead to ease of cooking and best results:

☆ Heat wok before adding oil.

☆ Have all ingredients needed for the recipe prepared and at hand before beginning to cook. Care should be taken in the preparation of the food so that everything cooks in a short time and adds to the appearance of the final dish.

☆ Any sauces or seasonings should generally be prepared in advance.

☆ Slice meat and poultry very thinly and evenly (it will slice easier if partially frozen and a very sharp knife is used).

☆ Ingredients that take the longest to cook should be put into the wok first.

☆ Add a small amount of food at a time – in batches if necessary.

☆ Ensure everything is ready for serving, including family or guests, as the food must be eaten as soon as it is cooked. It is not the sort of cooking that can be done ahead of time.

**Deep frying.** Points to note when cooking with oil:

☆ Care must be taken not to move or tilt the wok when it contains hot oil.

☆ Ensure wok is uncovered when heating oil.

☆ Ensure handles are not sticking over edge of stove.

☆ Be careful if adding moist food as it tends to spatter.

☆ After cooking, allow oil to cool before pouring out or returning to its container.

**Steaming and Braising.** Points to note when steaming and braising:

☆ During cooking some steam will condense and form drops of water under the domed lid. To shield the food, cover with a piece of aluminum foil.

☆ Check the water level once in a while and add more as needed.

A few well-chosen ingredients, now readily available, will give you the authentic flavors for many a delicious Oriental dish, enabling you to savor the pleasures of exotic Eastern cuisine.

Though the wok is primarily an Oriental utensil, I have interspersed the Eastern dishes with a variety of Western-style recipes, since wok cooking adapts well to many types of cuisine.

# Soups and Appetizers

## Wonton Soup

| | |
|---|---|
| **PREPARATION TIME:** | 15 minutes |
| **COOKING TIME:** | 15 minutes |
| **SERVES:** | 4 people |

*8oz ground pork*
*4 green onions, chopped finely*
*½ tsp finely chopped ginger root*
*1 tbsp light soy sauce*
*4oz wonton wrappers*
*1 tsp cornstarch*
*1 tsp sesame oil*
*1 tsp Chinese wine, or dry sherry*
*1 tsp sugar*
*Salt*
*Pepper*
*5 cups chicken stock*
*½ tsp sesame oil*

**Garnish**
*Coriander, or finely chopped green*
*onion*

Place in a bowl the ground pork, green onions, ginger, soy sauce, 1 tsp sesame oil, Chinese wine, sugar, cornstarch, salt and pepper. Mix together well and set aside. Heat stock in wok and bring to the boil. Season with salt and pepper. Wrap ½ teaspoon of pork mixture into each wonton wrapper. Close tightly and drop into stock. Cook for 5 minutes. Wontons will usually rise to the surface when cooked. Add ½ tsp sesame oil and stir in. Garnish with green onion or fresh coriander. Serve hot.

## Chinese Combination Soup

| | |
|---|---|
| **PREPARATION TIME:** | 30 minutes |
| **COOKING TIME:** | 20 minutes |
| **SERVES:** | 4 people |

*4 dried Chinese mushrooms*
*8oz chicken*
*4oz fine/thread egg noodles*
*1 clove garlic, sliced thinly*
*1 tsp finely sliced root ginger*
*¼ small cabbage, shredded*
*2½ cups chicken stock*
*1 tbsp peanut oil*
*2 eggs, beaten*
*1 tbsp dark soy sauce*
*1 tbsp sherry*
*1 tbsp water*

*1 tsp cornstarch*
*2 shallots, peeled and sliced finely*

Soak mushrooms in hot water for 20 minutes. Remove and discard stems. Slice mushroom caps thinly. Soak noodles in boiling salted water for 2 minutes. Rinse in cold water. Drain. Slice chicken finely. Heat wok and add peanut oil. Add garlic and ginger, and fry gently for 5 minutes, then discard. Add chicken, and fry for a few minutes until meat has turned white. Add mushrooms, shallots, cabbage and stock. Bring to the boil and simmer for 5 minutes. Gradually pour in eggs and stir so that they cook in shreds. Mix cornstarch with 1 tbsp of water, and pour into soup, stirring continuously. Cook for 2 minutes or until soup thickens.

Add noodles, soy sauce and sherry. Serve immediately.

**This page: Wonton Soup (top) and Curry Soup with Meatballs (bottom).**

**Facing page: Chinese Combination Soup (top) and Eggflower Soup (bottom).**

## Curry Soup with Meatballs

**PREPARATION TIME:** 30 minutes
**COOKING TIME:** 20 minutes
**SERVES:** 4 people

### Meatballs
8oz lean ground beef
1 clove garlic, crushed
1 onion, peeled and chopped finely
½ tsp salt
½ tsp curry powder
½ tsp ground cinnamon
½ tsp ground cloves
½ tsp ground pepper
2 tbsps breadcrumbs
1 small egg, lightly beaten

### Broth
1 tsp garam masala
1 tsp turmeric
2½ cups water
1 clove garlic, crushed
1 onion, peeled and finely chopped
1 tsp curry leaves
½ cup desiccated coconut, soaked in
  1 cup hot water for 15 minutes
2 tbsps peanut oil

Mix together meatball ingredients, and form into small balls about the size of walnuts. Heat wok, add oil and, when hot, fry meatballs. When browned well all over, remove with a slotted spoon, and drain on paper towels. Carefully drain oil from wok. Add 1 tsp of oil, and fry spices for 30 seconds. Add onion, curry leaves, and garlic, and cook together for 3 minutes. Meanwhile, strain coconut in a strainer, press out as much liquid as possible, and discard the pulp. Add water and coconut milk to the wok and simmer together for 5 minutes. Adjust seasoning. Strain soup and return to wok. Add meatballs and simmer a further 5 minutes. Serve hot.

## Hot and Sour Soup

**PREPARATION TIME:** 30 minutes
**COOKING TIME:** 30 minutes
**SERVES:** 4 people

4oz lean pork fillet
4 dried Chinese mushrooms
⅓ cup bamboo shoots, sliced
1 square beancurd, diced
2 tbsps sunflower or vegetable oil
5 cups light, clear stock, or hot water
  plus 2 chicken bouillon cubes
1 tsp cornstarch
2 tbsps cold water
1 tsp sesame oil

### Marinade
1 tbsp light soy sauce
3 tbsps brown vinegar
2 tbsps water
1 tsp sesame oil
Salt
Pepper

### Garnish
Fresh coriander

Soak Chinese mushrooms for 20 minutes in hot water. Meanwhile, slice pork into thin slivers. Make the marinade by combining light soy sauce, brown vinegar, water, sesame oil, and salt and pepper. Pour over pork and leave for 30 minutes. Drain mushrooms. Remove and discard stalks. Slice caps very finely. Remove pork from marinade, and reserve marinade. Heat wok, and add sunflower or vegetable oil. When hot, stir-fry pork, mushrooms and bamboo shoots for 2 minutes. Add stock and bring to the boil. Simmer for 10 minutes. Add beancurd, marinade, and salt and pepper to taste. Slake cornstarch in 2 tbsps of cold water. Add to soup and allow to simmer for 5 minutes. Add sesame oil and sprinkle with fresh coriander. Serve hot.

## Chicken and Asparagus Soup

**PREPARATION TIME:** 10 minutes
**COOKING TIME:** 45 minutes
**SERVES:** 4 people

1lb chicken pieces
1 onion, peeled and chopped roughly
1 carrot, chopped roughly
1 stick celery, chopped roughly
4 peppercorns
10oz can asparagus pieces
5 cups water
Salt
Pepper

### Garnish
Chopped parsley

Remove chicken meat from bones and cut into fine shreds. Put chicken bones, onion, carrot, celery, peppercorns and water in wok, and season with salt and pepper. Bring to the boil, reduce heat, and simmer for 30 minutes. Strain and return stock to wok. Add chicken shreds, and simmer until chicken is cooked. Add undrained asparagus pieces. Adjust seasoning. Serve sprinkled with chopped parsley.

## Eggflower Soup

**PREPARATION TIME:** 10 minutes
**COOKING TIME:** 10 minutes
**SERVES:** 4 people

2½ cups chicken stock
2 eggs, lightly beaten
1 tbsp light soy sauce
1¾ cups canned plum tomatoes
2 green onions, chopped finely

Drain and chop tomatoes, removing seeds, and reserve juice. Bring soy sauce, tomato juice and stock to the boil in the wok. Add tomatoes and half the green onions, and cook for 2 minutes. Dribble beaten eggs in gradually, stirring continuously. Serve immediately, sprinkled with remaining green onions.

Chicken and Asparagus
Soup (below) and Hot and
Sour Soup (right).

cooking. Use a slotted spoon to remove, and drain on paper towels. If necessary, store in an airtight container until needed.

## Chicken Liver Pâté

**PREPARATION TIME:** 20 minutes

**COOKING TIME:** 20 minutes

**SERVES:** 4 people as a starter

*8oz chicken livers, trimmed*
*1 cup butter*
*1 medium onion, peeled and chopped finely*
*1 bay leaf*
*1 clove garlic, crushed*
*1 tbsp brandy*
*1 tsp Worcestershire sauce*
*Salt*
*Pepper*

**Garnish**
*Sprig of parsley*

Heat wok and add half of the butter. Add onion, garlic and bay leaf, and fry gently until onion is soft but not colored. Increase heat, and add chicken livers and salt and freshly-ground black pepper to taste, and fry for 5 minutes, turning regularly. Add Worcestershire sauce and stir well. Remove from heat, and set aside to cool. Meanwhile, cream remaining butter. Remove bay leaf and chop liver finely – this can be done in a blender. Push through a strainer; beat in creamed butter and stir in brandy. Fill into individual ramekin dishes or into a china dish. If keeping, smooth over surface and cover with clarified butter. Garnish with a sprig of parsley.

## Cheese Nibbles

**PREPARATION TIME:** 20 minutes

**COOKING TIME:** 20 minutes

**MAKES:** 40 pieces

*½ cup Gruyère cheese*
*½ cup Emmenthal cheese*
*1 egg, lightly beaten*
*2 tbsps milk*
*1 tsp dry mustard*
*1 clove garlic, crushed*

## Poppadums

**COOKING TIME:** 5 minutes

*Poppadums*
*Oil for deep frying*

Heat oil in wok. When oil is hot, deep fry 1 poppadum at a time for 2-3 seconds, holding edges apart with forks. They will puff up, and should be pale golden in color. If browning, reduce heat of oil. If not cooking quickly enough, increase heat. Remove, shaking off excess oil, and drain on paper towels. They may be eaten immediately, or when cool may be kept in an airtight container until needed.

## Fried Bananas

**PREPARATION TIME:** 5 minutes

**COOKING TIME:** 10 minutes

**SERVES:** 4 people

*3-4 bananas*
*1 tbsp lemon juice*
*2 tbsps oil*
*Salt*

Peel bananas and slice diagonally. Heat wok and add oil. When hot, add bananas. Fry, turning carefully until browned well all over. Sprinkle with lemon juice and a pinch of salt, and serve as an accompaniment to a curry.

## Shrimp Crisps/Crackers (Krupuk)

**COOKING TIME:** 5 minutes

*Shrimp Crisps*
*Oil for deep frying*

Heat oil in wok, and make sure the oil is hot, but not too hot. It should be hot enough to puff the shrimp crisps in 2-3 seconds: if they brown, the oil is too hot. If it is not hot enough, they will take too long to cook, and will be tough and chewy. A few can be fried together, but do not put too many in as they need to be removed quickly before over-

This page: **Shrimp Crisps/ Crackers (top left), Fried Bananas (center right) and Poppadums (bottom).**

Facing page: **Chicken Liver Pâté (top) and Cheese Nibbles (bottom).**

## Seafood Hot and Sour Soup

**PREPARATION TIME:** 20 minutes

**COOKING TIME:** 20 minutes

**SERVES:** 4 people

2 dried Chinese mushrooms
1 cake fresh beancurd, diced
4oz shrimp, shelled and de-veined
2½ cups light stock, preferably fish stock
½ cup crab meat, or 2 crab-sticks, cut into ½" slices
1 tbsp oyster sauce
1 tbsp light soy sauce
1 tbsp lemon juice
½ tsp lemon rind, cut into slivers
1 tbsp vegetable oil
1 red chili pepper, seeds removed, and finely sliced
2 green onions, sliced
Salt
Pepper
1 tsp sesame oil

**Garnish**
*Fresh coriander, if desired*

Soak mushrooms in hot water and set aside for 20 minutes. Heat wok, add vegetable oil and, when hot, stir-fry shrimp, chili pepper, lemon rind and green onions. Add stock, oyster sauce and light soy sauce, and bring to the boil. Reduce heat and simmer for 5 minutes. Add salt and pepper to taste. Remove hard stalks from mushrooms and slice caps finely. Add crab meat, beancurd and Chinese mushrooms to wok, and cook a further 5 minutes. Stir in lemon juice and sesame oil. Adjust seasoning, and serve sprinkled with fresh coriander leaves if desired.

## Spring Rolls (Egg Rolls)

**PREPARATION TIME:** 20 minutes

**COOKING TIME:** 30 minutes

**MAKES:** 12 rolls

8oz finely ground pork
1 red chili pepper, seeds removed, and sliced finely
10 canned water chestnuts, chopped
1 onion, peeled and chopped finely
1 clove garlic, crushed
½ tsp grated ginger root
1 tsp ground turmeric
2 tbsps peanut oil
12 spring roll (egg roll) wrappers
Salt
Pepper
Peanut or vegetable oil for deep frying

Heat wok, add 2 tbsps of peanut oil, and fry garlic, ginger, ground

---

2 tbsps flour
1 tsp baking powder
Salt
Pepper
10 slices stale whole-wheat bread
Oil for deep frying

Sift together flour, baking powder,

mustard, and a pinch of salt and pepper. Grate cheese. Mix together cheese, egg, milk, garlic and flour mixture. Beat together well. Trim off bread-crusts, and cut each slice diagonally into 4 triangles. Spread one heaped teaspoon of mixture on each triangle of bread to cover well.

Heat oil in wok. When hot, carefully fry in batches with bread side up first. Deep fry until golden brown on both sides. Remove and drain on paper towels. Keep hot until all frying is completed. Serve hot.

Facing page: Seafood Hot
and Sour Soup (top) and
Corn and Chicken Soup
(bottom).

This page: Shrimp Toast
(top) and Spring Rolls (Egg
Rolls) (right).

turmeric and onion for 3 minutes. Add pork, and stir-fry until pork is browning. Add water chestnuts and chili pepper, and salt and pepper to taste, and fry for a further 2 minutes. Remove from wok, and set aside to cool. Place spring roll wrapper with one corner pointing towards you. Spoon some of the mixture just in front of the center. Fold over the corner nearest to you, and roll to center. Fold the two side points into the center and finish rolling up. They may be sealed with a paste of water and flour if necessary. Refrigerate until needed. Heat oil for deep frying in wok, and deep fry spring rolls in batches just before needed. Drain on paper towels, and serve warm with chilli or sweet-and-sour sauce.

## Shrimp Toast

| PREPARATION TIME: 15 minutes |
| COOKING TIME: 15 minutes |
| MAKES: approximately 20 pieces |

*8oz shrimp, shelled and de-veined, and chopped finely*
*1 small egg, beaten*
*2 tsps sherry*
*2 tsps oyster sauce*
*½ tsp grated ginger root*
*2 tsp cornstarch*
*Salt*
*5 slices white bread*
*Oil for deep frying*

Combine shrimp, beaten egg, sherry, oyster sauce, grated ginger, cornstarch and a pinch of salt. Using a 1½" round pastry cutter, cut out circles of bread. Spread mixture on each piece of bread to cover well. Heat oil in wok for deep frying. Fry in batches with bread side up first, until bread is golden brown. Remove and drain on paper towels. Keep hot until all frying is completed.

## Corn and Chicken Soup

| PREPARATION TIME: 15 minutes |
| COOKING TIME: 45 minutes |
| SERVES: 4 people |

*1 chicken, with giblets*
*1 8oz can cream style corn*
*1 onion, peeled and chopped roughly*
*1 carrot, scraped and chopped roughly*

*1 stick celery, chopped*
*6 peppercorns*
*Parsley stalks*
*1 bay leaf*
*5 cups water*
*Salt*
*Pepper*

**Garnish**
*Chopped parsley or chives*

Clean chicken, and cut into quarters. Put into wok with giblets, chopped vegetables, peppercorns, bay leaf, parsley stalks, seasoning and water. Bring to the boil. Reduce heat and simmer for 30 minutes. Strain and return stock to wok. Remove meat from chicken and cut into fine shreds. Add undrained corn to stock, and bring to boil. Simmer for 5 minutes. Add chicken and cook for 1 minute. Sprinkle with chopped parsley or chives. Serve hot.

## Rice Paper Shrimp Parcels

| PREPARATION TIME: 15 minutes |
| COOKING TIME: 15 minutes |
| MAKES: about 20 parcels |

*8oz shrimp, shelled and de-veined*
*6 green onions, sliced finely*
*1 packet rice paper*
*1 egg white*
*½ tsp cornstarch*
*⅔ cup peanut oil*
*1 tsp Chinese wine, or 2 tsps dry sherry*
*1 tsp light soy sauce*
*1 tsp sugar*
*Salt*
*Pepper*

Dry prepared shrimp on paper towels. Mix egg white, cornstarch, wine, sugar, soy sauce, green onions and seasoning together. Mix in

shrimp. Heat peanut oil in wok until hot. Wrap five or six shrimp in each piece of rice paper. Gently drop in rice paper parcels and deep fry for about 5 minutes. Serve hot.

## Crab Rolls

| PREPARATION TIME: 20 minutes |
| COOKING TIME: 20 minutes |
| MAKES: 12 rolls |

*1 cup crab meat, fresh or canned*
*3 green onions, finely sliced*
*12 spring roll (egg roll) wrappers*
*1oz cellophane noodles*
*¼ tsp grated ginger root*
*1 tsp oyster sauce*
*2 tbsps finely chopped bamboo shoots*
*Salt*
*Vegetable or peanut oil for deep frying*

Soak cellophane noodles in hot water for 8 minutes, or as directed, and drain. Flake crab meat, and drain if necessary. Combine crab meat with green onions, noodles, ginger, bamboo shoots, oyster sauce and salt to taste. Place spring roll wrappers with one corner pointing towards you. Spoon some of the mixture just before the center. Fold over the corner nearest you and roll to center. Fold the two side points into the center, and roll up completely. They may be sealed with a paste of flour and water if necessary. Refrigerate until needed. Heat oil in wok and deep fry batches of spring rolls just before serving. Drain on paper towels. Serve warm with ginger sauce or sweet-and-sour sauce.

**This page: Crab Rolls (top) and Rice Paper Shrimp Parcels (bottom).**

**Facing page: Ginger Scallops in Oyster Sauce (top) and Crispy Fish with Chili (bottom).**

# Fish and Seafood

## Crispy Fish with Chili

**PREPARATION TIME:** 40 minutes
**COOKING TIME:** 30 minutes
**SERVES:** 4 people

lb fish fillets, skinned, bones
  removed, and cut into 1″ cubes

**Batter**
tbsps flour
egg, separated
tbsp oil
tbsps milk
alt

**Sauce**
sp grated ginger root
tsp chili powder
tbsps tomato paste
tbsps tomato relish
tbsps dark soy sauce
tbsps Chinese wine or dry sherry
tbsps water
sp sugar
red chili pepper, seeds removed, and
  sliced finely
clove garlic, crushed
alt
pper
il for deep frying

ft the flour with a pinch of salt.
ake a well in the center, and drop
 the egg yolk and oil. Mix to a
nooth batter with the milk,
adually incorporating the flour.
eat well. Cover and set aside in a
ol place for 30 minutes. Whisk
g white until stiff, and fold into
tter just before using. Heat oil in
ok. Dip fish pieces into batter and
at completely. When oil is hot,
refully lower fish pieces in and
ok until cooked through and
lden brown – about 10 minutes.
emove with a slotted spoon.
eheat oil and refry each fish piece
r 2 minutes. Remove with a
otted spoon and drain on paper
wels. Carefully remove all but
bsp of oil from wok. Heat oil, and
d chili pepper, ginger, garlic, chili
owder, tomato paste, tomato
lish, soy sauce, sugar, wine and
ater, and salt and pepper to taste.
ir well over heat for 3 minutes.
crease heat and toss in fish pieces.
oat with sauce and, when heated
rough, serve immediately.

Place in a warm serving dish and serve hot with rice.

## Ginger Scallops in Oyster Sauce

**PREPARATION TIME:** 10 minutes

**COOKING TIME:** 15 minutes

**SERVES:** 4 people

1lb scallops, cleaned, dried on
 absorbent paper, and sliced
10 green onions, sliced diagonally
 into 1" slices
1" green ginger, peeled and sliced ver
 thinly
Salt
2 tbsps vegetable oil

**Sauce**

1 tbsp oyster sauce
1 tbsp light soy sauce
½ tsp sesame oil
1 tsp grated root ginger
1 tsp cornstarch
5 tbsps light stock, or 5 tbsps hot
 water and half a chicken bouillon
 cube
Pinch of sugar

Combine oyster sauce, soy sauce, sesame oil, cornstarch, sugar and grated ginger and set aside. Sprinkl the scallops with a pinch of salt. Heat wok, and add oil. Add sliced ginger and green onions, and stir-fr gently for 1 minute. Raise heat to high. Add scallops and stir-fry for 1 minute. Add sauce mixture and stir in. Remove from heat, and stir in stock gradually. Return to heat and bring to the boil, stirring continuously. Simmer gently for 3 minutes, until sauce is slightly thickened. Adjust seasoning. Serve immediately with boiled rice.

## Steamed Fish with Black Beans

**PREPARATION TIME:** 15 minutes

**COOKING TIME:** 15 minutes

**SERVES:** 4 people

2lbs whole snapper, or bass, cleaned
 and scaled
1 tbsp salted black beans
2 cloves garlic, crushed
1 tbsp light soy sauce
1 tsp Chinese wine, or 2 tsps dry
 sherry
1 tsp sugar
½ tsp cornstarch
1 tsp sesame oil
½ can bamboo shoots, cut into shred
Salt
Pepper

## Squid with Broccoli and Cauliflower

**PREPARATION TIME:** 15 minutes

**COOKING TIME:** 20 minutes

**SERVES:** 4 people

1lb squid, cleaned
1 onion, peeled and chopped roughly
8oz fresh broccoli flowerets
8oz fresh cauliflower flowerets
2 sticks celery, sliced diagonally
½ tsp grated ginger root
1 tbsp cornstarch
2 tbsps water
2 tbsps light soy sauce
2 tbsps Chinese wine, or dry sherry
2 tbsps oyster sauce
½ tsp sesame oil
½ tsp sugar
⅔ cup oil, for deep frying
Salt
Pepper

Cut cleaned squid lengthwise down center. Flatten out with inside uppermost. With a sharp knife make a lattice design, cutting deep into squid flesh (to tenderize and make squid curl when cooking). Heat oil in wok. Add squid and cook until it curls. Remove from pan and drain on paper towels. Carefully pour off all but 1 tbsp of oil. Add onion, celery, broccoli, cauliflower and ginger, and stir-fry for 3 minutes. Slake cornstarch with water, and add soy sauce, wine, oyster sauce, sesame oil, sugar, and salt and pepper to taste. Mix well and add to wok. Bring to the boil and simmer for 3 minutes, stirring continuously. Return squid and cook until heated through.

Facing page: Squid with Broccoli and Cauliflower.

This page: Singapore Fried Noodles (below) and Steamed Fish with Black Beans (bottom).

Wash and clean fish well and dry with paper towels. Make 3 or 4 diagonal cuts in flesh of fish on each side. Rub garlic into cuts and place fish on a heat-proof dish. Rinse black beans in cold water, then crush with the back of a spoon. Add cornstarch, sesame oil, soy sauce, sugar and wine, and salt and pepper and mix together well. Pour over fish. Sprinkle bamboo shoots on top of fish. Put plate on top of a bamboo steamer or metal trivet standing in wok. Add water, ensuring the level is below the level of the plate. Cover and bring to the boil. Steam for about 10 minutes after boiling point is reached. Ensure that the fish is cooked, but do not oversteam. Serve hot.

## Stir-Fried Shrimp and Pea Pods

**PREPARATION TIME:** 5 minutes

**COOKING TIME:** 5 minutes

**SERVES:** 4 people

*8oz shrimp, shelled and de-veined*
*4oz pea pods, trimmed*
*4 tbsps peanut oil*
*2 tbsps dry white wine*
*Juice of half a lemon*
*1 tbsp light soy sauce*
*Pinch of salt*
*Black pepper*

**Garnish**
*Parsley*

Blanch pea pods in boiling salted water for 1 minute. Drain and set aside. Heat wok, add the peanut oil, and stir-fry shrimp for 30 seconds. Add pea pods, dry white wine, lemon juice, soy sauce, and salt and pepper, and toss together until heated through. Adjust seasoning and garnish with parsley. Serve immediately with boiled rice.

## Seafood Combination

**PREPARATION TIME:** 20 minutes

**COOKING TIME:** 20 minutes

**SERVES:** 4 people

*8oz shrimp, shelled and de-veined*
*4oz squid, cleaned, cut into 1" rings, opened up, and scored with lattice design*
*4oz pea pods, trimmed*
*4oz white fish fillets, cut into 1" cubes*

*1 stick celery, sliced diagonally*
*1 carrot, scraped and cut into matchstick strips*
*1 tsp grated ginger root*
*½ tsp salt*
*1 tbsp dry white wine*
*1 egg white*
*1 tsp cornstarch*
*Oil for deep frying*

Combine wine, salt, egg white, grated ginger and cornstarch and mix well. Add shrimp and fish, and toss well. Drain shrimp and fish, reserving sauce. Blanch pea pods in boiling water for 1 minute. Drain. Heat oil in wok. Deep fry shrimp, fish and squid for 2 minutes. Remove from pan and drain on

**This page: Seafood Combination.**

**Facing page: Mediterranean Fish Stew (top) and Stir-Fried Shrimp and Pea Pods (bottom).**

paper towels. Carefully remove oil from wok, reserving 1 tbsp of oil in wok. Heat oil. Stir-fry carrot and celery for 3 minutes. Add pea pods and stir-fry a further 3 minutes. Add any remaining sauce and stir. Add seafood and toss well until heated through.

## Honey Sesame Shrimp

**PREPARATION TIME:** 20 minutes

**COOKING TIME:** 20 minutes

**SERVES:** 4 people

*1lb shrimp, shelled and de-veined*
*2 tbsps cornstarch*
*¾ cup flour*
*½ tsp baking powder*
*1 egg, lightly beaten*
*Pinch of salt*
*Pepper*
*⅔ cup water*
*Oil for deep frying*
*2 tbsps honey*
*1 tbsp sesame seeds*
*1 tbsp sesame oil*

Sift flour, baking powder and salt and pepper into a bowl. Make a well in the center and add egg and water, gradually bringing in the flour. Beat to a smooth batter and set aside for 10 minutes. Meanwhile, toss shrimp in cornstarch and coat well. Shake off any excess cornstarch. Add shrimp to batter and coat well. Heat oil in wok, and add shrimp, a few at a time. Cook until batter is golden. Remove and drain on paper towels, and keep warm. Repeat until all shrimp have been fried. Carefully remove hot oil from wok. Gently heat sesame oil in pan. Add honey and stir until mixed well and heated through. Add shrimp to mixture and toss well. Sprinkle over sesame seeds and again toss well. Serve immediately.

## Steamed Fish in Ginger

**PREPARATION TIME:** 20 minutes

**COOKING TIME:** 15 minutes

**SERVES:** 4 people

*3lbs whole snapper, bass or bream, cleaned and scaled*

**Stuffing**
*½ cup cooked rice*
*1 tsp grated root ginger*
*3 green onions, sliced finely*
*2 tsps light soy sauce*
*6 green onions, cut into 2" lengths, then into fine shreds*
*3 pieces green ginger, cut into fine shreds*

**Garnish**
*Lemon slices and parsley, if desired*

Mix together rice, grated ginger, sliced green onion and soy sauce. Stuff rice mixture into cleaned fish cavity, packing in well. Place fish on a heat-proof plate, and arrange strips of green onion and green ginger on top of fish. Put the plate on top of a bamboo steamer or metal trivet standing in wok. Add water, ensuring the water level is not up to the plate. Cover and bring to the boil. Steam for 10 minutes from boiling point. Ensure that the fish is cooked, but be sure not to oversteam the fish. Serve hot, garnished with lemon slices and parsley, if desired.

## Singapore Fried Noodles

**PREPARATION TIME:** 20 minutes

**COOKING TIME:** 25 minutes

**SERVES:** 4 people

*8oz packet egg noodles*
*8oz shrimp, shelled and de-veined*
*1 chicken breast, cut into shreds*
*1½ cups bean sprouts*
*2 cloves garlic, crushed*
*3 sticks celery, sliced diagonally*
*2 green onions, sliced*
*1 red chili pepper, seeds removed, and sliced*
*1 green chili pepper, seeds removed, and sliced*
*1 tsp chili powder*
*2 eggs, lightly beaten*
*3 tbsps oil*
*Salt*
*Pepper*

**Garnish**
*Chili flowers (carefully cut end of chili pepper into shreds, and soak in cold water until flower opens)*

Soak noodles in boiling water for 8 minutes, or as directed. Drain noodles on paper towels and leave to dry. Heat wok, and add 1 tbsp of oil. Add lightly beaten eggs, and salt and pepper to taste. Stir gently and cook until set. Remove from wok, and cut into thin strips and keep warm. Add remaining oil to wok. When hot, add garlic and chili powder and fry for 30 seconds. Add chicken, celery, green onions and red and green chili peppers, and stir-fry for 8 minutes or until chicken has cooked through. Add noodles, shrimp and bean sprouts, and toss until well mixed and heated through. Serve with scrambled egg strips on top and garnish with chili flowers.

## Mediterranean Fish Stew

**PREPARATION TIME:** 20 minutes

**COOKING TIME:** 30 minutes

**SERVES:** 4 people

*1lb white fish fillets, cut into 2" cubes*
*2 tbsps olive oil*
*2 cloves garlic, crushed*
*1 onion, peeled and sliced finely*
*2 sticks celery, sliced*
*1 tbsp chopped parsley*
*1 tsp oregano*
*2 tbsps tomato paste*
*⅔ cup fish stock or water*
*2 tbsps sweet Italian vermouth, or sweet sherry*
*4oz squid (optional), cleaned*
*2 leeks, white parts sliced finely*
*1¾ cups canned plum tomatoes*
*½ cup flat mushrooms, sliced*
*Salt*
*Pepper*

**Garnish**
*Lemon slices*
*Parsley*

Heat wok, and add oil. Add garlic, onion, celery, leeks, oregano, parsley and squid. Cover and cook gently for 10 minutes, stirring once or twice. Add tomato paste, stock or water, wine, undrained tomatoes, mushrooms, fish, and salt and pepper to taste. Bring to the boil, then cover and simmer gently for 15 minutes. Ensure fish is cooked through (it will be opaque all the way through, and will flake easily). Garnish with lemon slices and parsley. Serve immediately.

**Honey Sesame Shrimp (top) and Steamed Fish in Ginger (right).**

# Meat Dishes

## Pork with Black Bean Sauce

**PREPARATION TIME:** 40 minutes

**COOKING TIME:** 45 minutes

**SERVES:** 4 people

*8oz lean pork, cut into 1″ cubes*
*1 tbsp oil*
*1 red pepper, cored, seeds removed, and sliced*

**Sauce**
*3 tbsps black beans, rinsed in cold water and crushed with back of a spoon*
*2 tbsps Chinese wine, or dry sherry*
*1 tsp grated ginger*
*2 tbsps light soy sauce*
*3 cloves garlic, crushed*
*1 tbsp cornstarch*
*⅔ cup water*

Mix together black beans, wine, ginger, soy sauce and garlic. Blend cornstarch with 2 tbsps of water and add to mixture. Place pork in a bowl, and pour over sauce. Toss together well. Leave for at least 30 minutes. Heat wok, add oil and stir-fry red pepper for 3 minutes. Remove and set aside. Add pork, reserving marinade sauce. Stir-fry pork until browned well all over. Add marinade sauce and remaining water. Bring to the boil. Reduce heat, cover, and gently simmer for about 30 minutes, until pork is tender, stirring occasionally. Add more water if necessary. Just before serving, add red pepper and heat through. Serve with plain white rice.

## Lamb Meatballs with Yogurt

**PREPARATION TIME:** 15 minutes

**COOKING TIME:** 30 minutes

**SERVES:** 4 people

*1lb lean ground lamb*
*2 cloves garlic, crushed*
*1 small onion, peeled and grated*
*½ tsp chili powder*
*1 tsp garam masala*
*1 tbsp chopped mint*
*2 tbsps breadcrumbs*

*1 egg, lightly beaten*
*2 tbsps oil*
*½ cup plain yogurt*
*Small pinch of saffron strands, or ¼ tsp ground turmeric*
*2 tbsps boiling water*

*Salt*
*Pepper*

**Garnish**
*Fresh coriander or mint*

**This page: Beef and Oyster Sauce.**

**Facing page: Lamb Meatballs with Yogurt (top) and Pork with Black Bean Sauce (bottom).**

In a bowl, mix together ground lamb, garlic, onion, chili powder, garam masala, mint and breadcrumbs. Add lightly beaten egg to bind ingredients together. Add salt and pepper to taste. Wet hands. Take a teaspoon of mixture, and roll between palms, forming small balls. Heat wok and add oil. Add meatballs, shake wok to make meatballs roll around, and fry until browned well all over. Add saffron or turmeric to 2 tbsps boiling water. Leave for 5 minutes. Add water to yogurt, and stir in until evenly mixed. Reheat meatballs and serve on yogurt. Garnish with mint or fresh coriander. Serve with rice.

## Beef and Oyster Sauce

**PREPARATION TIME:** 30 minutes
**COOKING TIME:** 20 minutes
**SERVES:** 4 people

1lb sirloin or butt steak, sliced into thin strips
1½ cups bean sprouts
½ cup button mushrooms
1 red pepper, cored, seeds removed, and chopped roughly
2 sticks celery, sliced diagonally
2 onions, peeled and quartered
2 tbsps light soy sauce
2 tbsps peanut or vegetable oil

### Oyster Sauce
3 tbsps oyster sauce
1 chicken bouillon cube dissolved in 2 tbsps boiling water
1 tbsp dark soy sauce
1 tbsp Chinese wine or dry sherry
1 tbsp cornstarch
2 tbsps cold water
Salt
Pepper

Place steak in a bowl and pour over 2 tbsps light soy sauce. Toss together well and set aside for at least 30 minutes. Meanwhile, mix together oyster sauce, chicken stock, dark soy sauce and wine. Blend together cornstarch and cold water, and set aside. Heat wok, and add oil. Add onion, celery, mushrooms and red pepper, and stir-fry for 5 minutes. Remove from wok and set aside. Reheat oil and, when hot, toss in steak. Brown well all over, then add sauce and fried vegetables. Add cornstarch mixture and bring to the boil, tossing continuously. Add salt and pepper to taste. Finally, add bean sprouts and simmer gently for 3 minutes. Serve hot with noodles or rice.

## Sweet and Sour Pork with Peppers

**PREPARATION TIME:** 1 hour 15 minutes
**COOKING TIME:** 30 minutes
**SERVES:** 4 people

1lb pork tenderloin, cut into 1" cubes
1 large green pepper, cored, seeds removed, and chopped roughly
1 large yellow or red pepper, cored, seeds removed, and chopped roughly
1 small can or jar of Chinese mixed pickle
1 large onion, peeled and chopped finely
1¼ cups peanut oil

### Batter
1 egg
1 tsp peanut oil
¼ cup cornstarch
¼ cup flour
¼ tsp baking powder
Water

### Marinade
1 tbsp peanut oil
½ tsp light soy sauce
2 tsps Chinese wine, or 1 tbsp dry sherry
1 tsp cornstarch
1 tsp sugar
Pinch of salt
Pinch of pepper

### Sauce
¼ cup sugar
⅓ cup wine vinegar
⅓ cup water
1 tbsp tomato paste
Pinch of salt
1 tsp cornstarch
Few drops of red food coloring (if desired)

Mix together marinade ingredients. Pour over pork pieces and leave for about 1 hour, turning occasionally. Mix together batter ingredients, with enough water to form batter. Add pork. Heat peanut oil in wok. When hot, deep-fry pork pieces in small batches, so that they do not stick together. Remove when golden brown, using a slotted

spoon, and set aside. Continue until all battered pork pieces are cooked. Heat oil again and repeat process, cooking pork for 5 minutes to make batter nice and crisp. Keep warm. Carefully drain off all but 1 tbsp of oil. Heat, and add onion, peppers and Chinese mixed pickle. Cover and cook for 3 minutes. Remove and set aside. Heat vinegar, water, sugar, tomato paste, red food coloring and salt. Slake cornstarch with 1 tbsp of water. Stir into sauce. Bring to the boil and cook for 3 minutes. Add pork and vegetables to sauce. Serve hot with rice.

## Beef Worcestershire

**PREPARATION TIME:** 40 minutes
**COOKING TIME:** 20 minutes
**SERVES:** 4 people

1lb sirloin or butt steak, cut into 1½" cubes
2oz wonton wrappers
⅔ cup oil for deep frying

### Sauce
2 tbsps Worcestershire sauce
1 tbsp dark soy sauce
1 tbsp sugar
Pinch of salt
Pinch of pepper
½ tsp cornstarch

Mix together ingredients for sauce, and pour over steak. Toss well. Leave for at least 30 minutes, turning occasionally. Meanwhile, heat oil in wok. Fold wonton wrappers in half diagonally and seal open corners with water and press

**Beef Worcestershire (top right) and Sweet and Sour Pork with Peppers (right).**

together. Deep fry a few wonton wrappers at a time until golden brown. Remove with a slotted spoon and drain on paper towels. Repeat until there are enough wonton wrappers to go around the edge of the serving dish. Carefully remove all but 2 tbsps of oil from wok. Remove steak from sauce mixture and reserve. Heat wok, and when oil is hot, add steak and stir-fry until well browned. Pour over sauce and bring to the boil. Reduce heat and simmer, stirring continuously. When sauce thickens, and will coat steak well, place in warm serving dish and garnish with wonton wrappers. Serve immediately with boiled rice.

## Pork with Plum Sauce

| | |
|---|---|
| **PREPARATION TIME:** 40 minutes | |
| **COOKING TIME:** 30 minutes | |
| **SERVES:** 4 people | |

*1lb pork tenderloin, cut into 1" cubes*
*1 tbsp cornstarch*
*1 tsp sesame oil*

**This page: Beef with Mango.**

**Facing page: Pork with Plum Sauce (top) and Stir-Fried Leeks and Lamb (bottom).**

1 tbsp light soy sauce
1 tbsp sherry
1 tbsp brown sugar
½ tsp cinnamon
1 clove garlic, crushed
1 green onion, sliced finely
2 tbsps peanut oil
4 tbsps bottled plum sauce
¼ cup water
Salt
Pepper

## Garnish
*Green onion flowers*

Mix together cornstarch, sesame oil, light soy sauce, sherry, brown sugar, cinnamon and salt. Pour over pork, and toss together. Leave for at least 30 minutes. Remove pork and reserve marinade. Heat wok and add peanut oil. Add pork, and stir-fry until golden brown all over. Add green onion, plum sauce and water to wok, and mix together well. Bring to boil, cover, and simmer gently for 15 minutes, or until pork is tender, stirring occasionally. Add marinade, and bring to boil. Simmer gently for a further 5 minutes. Garnish with green onion flowers. (To make these, cut green onion into 2″ lengths. Carefully cut lengths into fine shreds, keeping one end intact, and then soak in cold water until curling.) Serve hot with boiled rice.

## Guy's Curry (Hot)

**PREPARATION TIME:** 40 minutes

**COOKING TIME:**
2 hours 15 minutes

**SERVES:** 4 people

2lbs steak, skirt or rump, cut into ½″ cubes
1½ cups coconut cream
1 onion, peeled and finely chopped
3 cloves garlic, chopped
2 tbsps golden raisins
1 tbsp curry leaves
1 dsp cumin
1 dsp coriander
1 tbsp vindaloo curry paste or powder (or milder if a curry less hot than vindaloo is desired)
1 carrot, grated
2 apples, chopped finely
1 banana, sliced finely
2 tomatoes, chopped finely
1 red pepper, cored, seeds removed, and chopped finely
6 small pieces lemon rind
2 tbsps desiccated coconut
2 tsps sugar
1 cup water
⅔ cup safflower or vegetable oil

## Accompaniments
1 apple, chopped finely
1 banana, sliced
1 red pepper, cored, seeds removed, and chopped finely
1 carrot, grated
1 tomato, chopped finely
2 tbsps golden raisins
2 tbsps desiccated coconut
Half a cucumber, sliced, in 2 tbsps natural yogurt

Prepare fruit and vegetables. Heat wok, add oil and heat until warm. Add onion and garlic, and fry until golden brown. Remove garlic, and discard. Add steak and stir-fry until well browned all over. Add sultanas and stir in well. Add curry leaves, stir in, and cook for 5 minutes. Add cumin and coriander and stir. Cook a further 5 minutes. Add curry powder or paste and cook for 10 minutes. Add grated carrot, red pepper, apples, tomatoes, lemon rind and banana and mix in well. Add water. Cover and cook for 30 minutes. Stir in desiccated coconut and cook for a further 30 minutes. Add sugar and cook for another 20 minutes. Add more water as necessary. Add coconut cream and cook a further 20 minutes. Serve hot with boiled rice and accompaniments.

## Stir-Fried Leeks and Lamb

**PREPARATION TIME:** 10 minutes

**COOKING TIME:** 30 minutes

**SERVES:** 4 people

1lb lamb, cut into 1″ cubes
1lb leeks, cut into 1″ slices
1 tsp rosemary
1 tsp redcurrant jelly
1 tbsp chopped mint
1 tsp basil
1 16oz can plum tomatoes
1 tbsp oil
Salt
Pepper

## Garnish
*Fresh mint*

Heat wok, and add oil. Add rosemary, basil and leeks, and stir-fry gently for 3 minutes. Remove from wok, and increase heat. Add lamb and stir-fry until well-browned all over. Return leeks to wok. Add undrained tomatoes, redcurrant jelly, mint, and salt and pepper to taste. Cover and simmer for 20 minutes, adding water if necessary. Serve hot, garnished with fresh mint.

**Right: Guy's Curry (Hot).**

# Devilled Kidneys

| PREPARATION TIME: |
|---|
| 1 hour 15 minutes |

| COOKING TIME: 20 minutes |
|---|

| SERVES: 4 people |
|---|

1lb veal kidneys
1 tbsp Worcestershire sauce
1 tbsp dark soy sauce
2 tbsps butter
1 tsp cornstarch
1 tbsp water

## Devilling Mixture
1 tsp salt
1 tsp sugar
½ tsp ground black pepper
½ tsp ground ginger
½ tsp dry mustard
¼ tsp curry powder

## Garnish
*Sprig of parsley*

Skin the kidneys and cut in half lengthwise. Mix the dry devilling mixture together, and coat kidneys well. Leave for at least 1 hour. Heat wok and melt butter. Brown the kidneys quickly in the hot butter. Add Worcestershire sauce and soy sauce, and bring to the boil. Cover and simmer for 15 minutes thickening with cornstarch mixed with water if necessary. Garnish with parsley and serve with saffron rice.

# Calves' Liver with Piquant Sauce

| PREPARATION TIME: 10 minutes |
|---|

| COOKING TIME: 25 minutes |
|---|

| SERVES: 4 people |
|---|

1lb calves' liver
1 onion, peeled and sliced
1 tbsp oil
2 tbsps butter
1 tbsp flour
1¼ cups brown stock, or 1¼ cups hot
    water and 1 beef bouillon cube
2 tbsps tomato, mango, or other fruit
    relish
1 tbsp tomato paste
1 clove garlic, crushed
1 tsp dry mustard, mixed with 2 tsps
    water
Salt
Pepper

## Garnish
*Chopped parsley*

Heat wok and add butter. When melted, stir in flour and cook until lightly browned. Remove from heat and gradually stir in stock. Return to heat and add tomato paste and garlic. Stir until boiling. Add mustard and salt and pepper to taste, and let simmer for 5 minutes. Add relish and mix well. Remove from wok and set aside. Meanwhile, slice liver very thinly. Wash and drain on paper towels. Heat wok and add oil. When hot add onion.

Fry gently over medium heat until just turning color. Add slices of liver in a single layer, and fry for about 3 minutes on each side, depending on thickness of slices. The liver should be cooked through and still tender. Do not overcook. Add piquant sauce to wok and toss together. Sprinkle with chopped parsley. Serve immediately on boiled rice.

**This page: Devilled Kidneys (top) and Calves' Liver with Piquant Sauce (bottom).**

**Facing page: Sweet and Sour Pork and Pineapple.**

steak and vegetables and mix well. Make seasoning sauce by mixing cornstarch with remaining 1 tbsp of light soy sauce, and adding 1 tsp of sugar. When well mixed, pour into wok and stir. Bring to the boil and cook for 3 minutes. Serve hot with rice.

## Braised Pork with Spinach and Mushrooms

**PREPARATION TIME:** 20 minutes

**COOKING TIME:** 30 minutes

**SERVES:** 4 people

*1lb pork tenderloin, cut into thin strips*
*8oz spinach leaves, washed, hard*
*  stalks removed, and shredded*
*4 dried Chinese mushrooms, soaked*
*  in hot water for 20 minutes, stems*
*  discarded, and caps sliced finely*
*½ tsp ground nutmeg*
*2 tbsps water*
*2 tbsps peanut oil*
*1 onion, peeled and quartered*
*1 clove garlic, crushed*
*1 tbsp flour*
*Salt*
*Pepper*

Heat wok, add 1 tsp of oil, and roll it around to coat the surface. Put nutmeg and spinach in wok, and cook gently for 5 minutes. Remove from pan. Add remaining oil to wok and fry garlic and onion over gentle heat for 5 minutes. Remove from wok. Meanwhile, add a good pinch of salt and freshly-ground black pepper to the flour and toss in the pork, coating well. Fry pork until each piece is browned all over. Add water and mushrooms, and return onion mixture to wok. Cover and simmer gently for 10 minutes, stirring occasionally. Add spinach and salt and pepper to taste, and cook, uncovered, for 2 minutes. Serve hot with steamed rice.

**This page: Braised Pork with Spinach and Mushrooms (top) and Steak with Black Bean Sauce (bottom).**

**Facing page: Steak Chinese Style (top) and Lamb Curry (Mild) (bottom).**

## Steak with Black Bean Sauce

**PREPARATION TIME:**
1 hour 15 minutes

**COOKING TIME:** 20 minutes

**SERVES:** 4 people

*8oz sirloin or butt steak, thinly sliced*
*1 large onion, peeled and chopped*
*1 large green pepper, cored, seeds*
*  removed, and diced*
*3 cloves garlic, crushed*
*1 tsp grated ginger root*
*1 small can sliced bamboo shoots,*
*  drained*
*3 tsps black beans*
*2 tbsps light soy sauce*
*4 tbsps peanut oil*
*1 tsp Chinese wine, or 2 tsps dry*
*  sherry*
*3 tsps sugar*
*1 tsp cornstarch*
*1 tsp sesame oil*
*Pinch of baking soda*
*Salt*
*Pepper*

Put sliced steak into a bowl, and sprinkle over baking soda. Add 1 tbsp of light soy sauce, 1 tsp of sugar, wine, sesame oil, salt and pepper, and leave to marinate for at least 1 hour. Heat wok and add 2 tbsps peanut oil. When hot, add steak and fry quickly. Remove from heat, and remove steak. Set aside. Add onion, green pepper, bamboo shoots, and a pinch of salt to wok. Cover and cook for 3 minutes. Remove and set aside. Make black bean sauce by crushing black beans and mixing with garlic, ginger, 1 tsp of sugar and 1 tbsp of peanut oil. Heat wok, add 1 tbsp of oil and pour in black bean mixture. Add

## Happys' Curry

**PREPARATION TIME:** 20 minutes

**COOKING TIME:** 30 minutes

**SERVES:** 4 people

1lb skirt or butt steak, cut into 1"
   cubes
8oz potatoes, peeled and diced
2 onions, peeled and chopped very
   finely
3 cloves garlic, crushed
1 tsp grated ginger root
1 tsp ground turmeric
½ tsp chili powder
1 tsp garam masala
½ tsp salt
1¼ cups water
¼ cup peanut oil

**Garnish**
Fresh coriander

Heat wok and add oil. Add ginger, garlic and onion, and fry gently for 5 minutes. Add turmeric, chili powder, garam masala and salt, and fry for 30 seconds. Add steak, and stir-fry until browned well all over. Add potatoes and water, and bring to the boil. Reduce heat, and cover. Simmer gently until meat is tender and potatoes are cooked. Garnish with fresh coriander and serve with rice if desired.

## Pork with Chili

**PREPARATION TIME:** 1 hour

**COOKING TIME:** 20 minutes

**SERVES:** 4 people

10oz pork tenderloin, cut into 1"
   cubes
1 green pepper, cored, seeds removed,
   and sliced
1 red chili pepper, seeds removed, and
   sliced finely
4 green onions, chopped
1 clove garlic, crushed
1 tsp sugar
1 tsp cornstarch
1 tsp peanut oil
1 tsp Chinese wine, or dry sherry
⅔ cup peanut oil, for deep frying

**Sauce**
1 tsp chili powder
2 tbsps dark soy sauce
1 tsp Worcestershire sauce
½ tsp five-spice powder
Pinch of salt

Mix together garlic, sugar, 1 tsp peanut oil, wine and cornstarch, and pour over pork. Cover and leave for at least 1 hour, turning occasionally. Meanwhile, combine ingredients for sauce in a bowl. Mix well. Set aside. Heat oil in wok until hot. Toss in pork cubes, and cook until golden brown and cooked through – about 10 minutes. Drain and set aside. Carefully remove all but 1 tbsp of oil from wok. Heat oil and add green pepper, chili pepper and green onions. Stir-fry for 2 minutes. Add sauce and pork, and bring to boil, stirring continuously. Adjust seasoning. Serve immediately with rice or noodles.

## Beef with Mango

**PREPARATION TIME:** 20 minutes

**COOKING TIME:** 15 minutes

**SERVES:** 4 people

1lb sirloin or butt steak, sliced thinly
1 can mangoes, drained, reserving
   ¼ cup mango juice
1 tsp sugar
½ tsp salt
1 tsp cornstarch
Pinch of pepper
2 tbsps mango chutney
1 tbsp plum sauce
1 tbsp oil

Combine 2 tbsps mango juice, sugar, cornstarch, salt and pepper, and pour over steak. Toss well and set aside for 15 minutes. Mix remaining mango juice with mango chutney and plum sauce, and set aside. Chop finely half of the mangoes and add to the sauce, retaining enough slices for decoration. Heat wok and add oil. Stir-fry steak for 5 minutes, tossing well, or until browned all over. Add mango-plum sauce and cook for a further 5 minutes. Decorate dish with reserved mango slices. Serve with rice.

## Steak Chinese Style

**PREPARATION TIME:**
1 hour 15 minutes

**COOKING TIME:** 20 minutes

**SERVES:** 4 people

8oz sirloin or butt steak, cut into
   1" pieces
1 can straw mushrooms, drained
2 green onions, sliced diagonally into
   ½" pieces
2 cloves garlic, crushed
1 can baby corn, drained
½ tsp crushed ginger
1 tbsp oyster sauce
1 tbsp light soy sauce
2 tbsps dark soy sauce
2 tsps sugar
1 tsp sesame oil
1 tsp Chinese wine, or 2 tsps dry
   sherry

1 tsp cornstarch
¼ cup water
Pinch of baking soda
3 tbsps peanut oil
Salt
Pepper

**Garnish**
Green onion flowers (cut green
   onions into 2" lengths. Carefully
   cut into fine shreds, keeping one
   end intact, and then soak in cold
   water until curling)

Put steak in a bowl and sprinkle over baking soda. Mix together light soy sauce, sesame oil, wine, half the sugar, half the cornstarch, and seasoning. Pour over the steak and leave for at least an hour, turning meat occasionally. Meanwhile, make sauce by mixing 2 tbsps of dark soy sauce, remaining sugar and cornstarch, and water. Mix together and set aside. Heat wok, add peanut oil and, when hot, fry steak for 4 minutes. Remove from wok and set aside. Add garlic, green onions, ginger, mushrooms, baby corn, and finally steak. Add oyster sauce, and mix well. Then add sauce mixture and bring to the boil. Cook for 3 minutes, stirring occasionally. Serve hot with rice, garnished with green onion flowers.

## Sweet and Sour Pork and Pineapple

**PREPARATION TIME:** 20 minutes

**COOKING TIME:** 45 minutes

**SERVES:** 4 people

1lb pork tenderloin, cut into 1" cubes
1 clove garlic, crushed
1 tsp grated ginger root
2 tbsps light soy sauce
1 tbsp cornstarch
2 tbsps peanut oil
⅔ cup water
2 tbsps white wine vinegar
2 tbsps tomato paste
1 tbsp sugar
1 can pineapple chunks, drained

**Garnish**
Fresh coriander

Place pork in bowl. Pour over light soy sauce and toss together. Leave for 15 minutes. Make sauce. Mix together vinegar, tomato paste and sugar, and set aside. Heat wok and add oil. Remove pork from soy sauce, and add soy sauce to sauce mixture. Toss pork in cornstarch, coating well. When oil is hot, brown pork well all over. Remove

from pan and reduce heat. Fry garlic and ginger for 30 seconds. Add water. Bring to the boil, then return pork to wok. Reduce heat; cover and simmer for 15 minutes, stirring occasionally. Add sauce mixture and pineapple, and simmer for a further 15 minutes. Garnish with coriander. Serve hot with rice or noodles.

## Lamb Curry (Mild)

**PREPARATION TIME:** 45 minutes
**COOKING TIME:** 1 hour
**SERVES:** 4 people

*2lb leg of lamb*
*2 tbsps plain yogurt*
*1 tbsp sesame oil*
*2 tsps garam masala*
*4 cloves garlic, crushed*
*1 tsp grated ginger*
*2 tsps curry powder*
*½ tsp ground black pepper*
*2 tbsps desiccated coconut*
*1 onion, peeled and sliced finely*
*1 tsp curry leaves*
*3 ripe tomatoes, chopped roughly*
*2 tbsps golden raisins*
*1 potato, peeled and chopped into ½" cubes*
*1 tsp sambal oelek*
*3 cups lamb stock*
*1 tbsp peanut oil*
*Salt*
*Pepper*

**Garnish**
*1 tbsp desiccated coconut*

Cut lamb into 1" cubes. Put bones in pan, cover with water, and bring to the boil. Simmer for 10 minutes. Strain and discard bones. Mix together yogurt, sesame oil, garam masala, garlic, ginger, curry powder, pepper and sambal oelek. Add lamb and toss well. Leave to marinate for 30 minutes. Heat wok, and add peanut oil. Fry onion and curry leaves. When softened, increase heat and add lamb and marinade. Brown lamb well. Add lamb stock, potato, tomatoes, desiccated coconut, raisins, and salt and pepper to taste. Bring to the boil. Reduce heat and cover, and cook gently for 20 minutes. Ensure potato is covered with liquid (add water if necessary). Remove cover, and cook for a further 15 minutes. Serve hot, sprinkled with desiccated coconut. Serve with boiled rice and poppadums.

## Pork Chow Mein

**PREPARATION TIME:** 20 minutes
**COOKING TIME:** 20 minutes
**SERVES:** 4 people

*10oz egg noodles*
*1lb pork, sliced thinly*
*1 tbsp Chinese wine, or dry sherry*
*1 tsp grated root ginger*
*1 leek, sliced*
*1 red pepper, cored, seeds removed, and cut into strips*
*1 stick celery, sliced diagonally*
*2 tbsps peas*
*⅔ cup chicken or light stock*
*1 tbsp light soy sauce*
*1 tsp sugar*
*1 tsp cornstarch*
*1 tbsp water*
*1 small can bamboo shoots, sliced*
*3 tbsps oil*
*Salt*
*Pepper*

Soak noodles in hot water for 8 minutes, or as directed. Rinse in cold water, and drain. Combine wine, soy sauce and sugar, and pour over pork. Toss together and set aside for at least 15 minutes. Heat wok and add oil. Add ginger, celery and leek, and stir-fry for 2 minutes. Add red pepper and bamboo shoots, and stir-fry for a further 2 minutes. Remove from wok. Increase heat, and add pork, reserving marinade. Stir-fry over high heat for 4 minutes. Return vegetables to wok. Add chicken stock gradually and stir well. Add peas and cook for 2 minutes. Blend cornstarch with water. Mix into marinade sauce and stir well. Add noodles and sauce to wok and toss together, heating through as sauce thickens. Add salt and pepper to taste. Simmer for 3 minutes. Serve hot.

**Pork Chow Mein (right).**

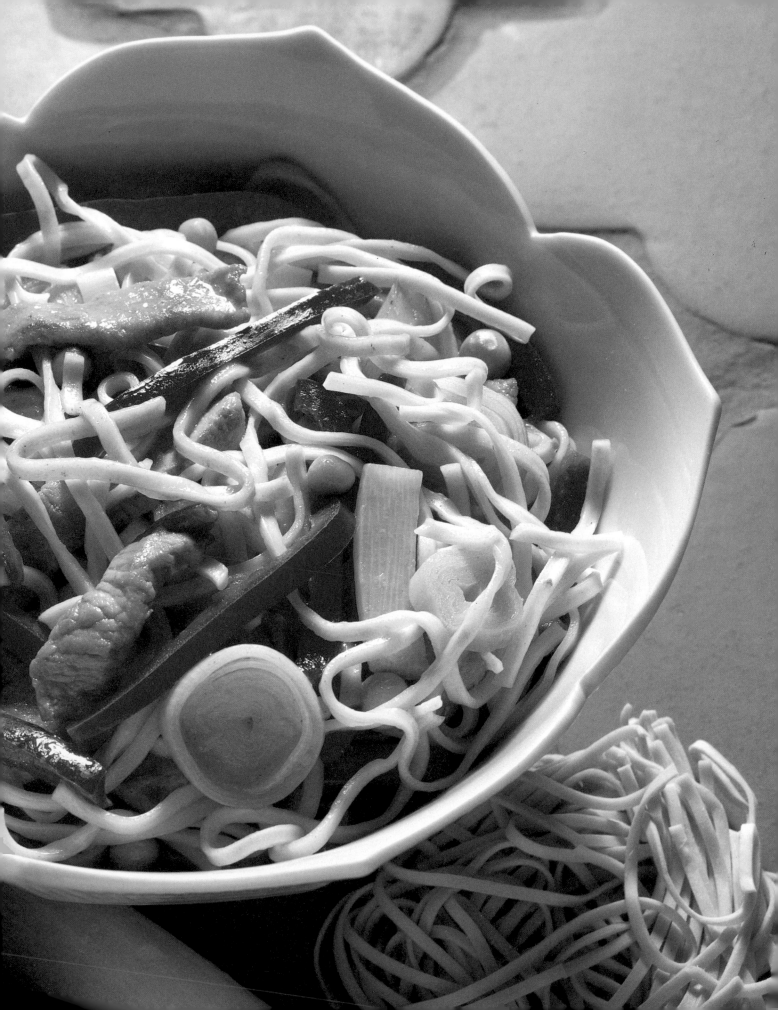

30 minutes. Make sauce. Heat wok, add half peanut oil and heat gently. Stir-fry peanuts for 2-3 minutes. Remove from wok, and drain on paper towels. Crush chili peppers, shallots and garlic to a smooth paste or blend. Grind peanuts to fine powder. Heat remaining oil in wok over a medium heat. Fry chili paste for 1-2 minutes. Add ⅔ cup water. Bring to the boil. Add peanuts, brown sugar, lemon juice and salt to taste. Stir until sauce is thick – approximately 10 minutes. Put in bowl, and keep warm. Heat wok, and add oil. Stir-fry meat until well browned all over. Serve with peanut sauce and boiled rice.

## Piquant Lambs' Livers

| | |
|---|---|
| **PREPARATION TIME:** | 15 minutes |
| **COOKING TIME:** | 20 minutes |
| **SERVES:** | 4 people |

*1lb lambs' livers, cut into thin strips*
*4 tbsps butter or margarine*
*2 tbsps wine vinegar*
*1 onion, peeled and sliced finely*
*⅓ cup white wine*
*1 tbsp chopped parsley*
*1 tbsp flour*
*Salt*
*Pepper*

**Garnish**
*Chopped parsley*

Combine flour with a good pinch of salt and freshly-ground black pepper. Toss in liver and coat well. Heat wok and add half the butter over gentle heat. Add onion and fry gently until transparent. Add vinegar and cook over high heat until vinegar has evaporated. Add remaining butter and when hot add liver. Stir-fry briskly for about 3 minutes. Add wine, parsley, and salt and pepper to taste. Bring to the boil and simmer for 5 minutes. Sprinkle with chopped parsley and serve with saffron rice.

## Steak with Peanut Sauce

| | |
|---|---|
| **PREPARATION TIME:** | 45 minutes |
| **COOKING TIME:** | 30 minutes |
| **SERVES:** | 4 people |

*1lb sirloin or butt steak, cut into ½" cubes*
*1 tbsp oil*

**Marinade**
*½ tsp chili powder*
*Juice of half a lemon*
*2 tsps brown sugar*
*½ tsp salt*
*1 tsp ground coriander*
*1 tsp ground cumin*

**Peanut Sauce**
*2 tbsps peanut oil*
*⅔ cup raw shelled peanuts*
*2 red chili peppers, seeds removed, and chopped (or 1 tsp chili powder)*
*2 shallots, chopped*
*1 clove garlic, crushed*
*1 tsp brown sugar*
*Juice of half a lemon*
*Salt*

Mix together marinade ingredients, and marinate steak for at least

**This page: Steak with Peanut Sauce (top) and Mee Goreng (bottom).**

**Facing page: Kidneys with Bacon (top) and Piquant Lambs' Livers (bottom).**

## Kidneys with Bacon

**PREPARATION TIME:** 20 minutes

**COOKING TIME:** 25 minutes

**SERVES:** 4 people

1lb lambs' kidneys
1 tbsp tomato relish
8 rashers bacon, diced
1 onion, peeled and quartered
3 cloves garlic, crushed
2 tbsps oil
1 tbsp light soy sauce
1 tbsp cornstarch
3 tbsps sherry
1 tbsp chopped parsley
2 tbsps water
Salt
Pepper

### Garnish
Sprig of parsley

Cut kidneys in half and remove hard core with a sharp knife or scissors. Cut a lattice design on back of kidneys. Pour over sherry, and set aside for 15 minutes. Heat wok and add oil. Add bacon, onion and garlic, and stir-fry for 5 minutes. Remove from wok. Add kidneys, reserving sherry, and fry for 3 minutes. Stir in tomato relish. Add soy sauce and water to wok, and return bacon and onion mixture. Add salt and pepper to taste. Cover and simmer gently for 10 minutes. Meanwhile, blend cornstarch with sherry marinade. Add parsley and cornstarch mixture, and stir, cooking gently until sauce thickens. Garnish with parsley. Serve hot with rice.

## Lamb with Cherries

**PREPARATION TIME:** 15 minutes

**COOKING TIME:**
1 hour 15 minutes

**SERVES:** 4 people

1lb boneless lamb from leg, cut into 1"
    cubes
2 tbsps butter or margarine
1 onion, peeled and chopped finely
½ tsp turmeric
½ tsp cinnamon
½ tsp ground nutmeg
1 tsp brown sugar
1 can black cherries, stoned
1 tbsp lemon juice
1 tbsp arrowroot or cornstarch
⅔ cup water
Salt
Pepper

Heat half butter in wok. Add lamb and fry quickly to brown well all over. Remove from wok and set aside. Add remaining butter and onion and fry for 2 minutes. Add turmeric, cinnamon, nutmeg and brown sugar, and fry for a further 1 minute. Add salt and pepper to taste. Return lamb to wok and add water. Cover and gently simmer for 45 minutes to 1 hour, until lamb is tender. And undrained cherries. Blend arrowroot or cornstarch with lemon juice and stir into mixture. Bring to boil and simmer for 4 minutes or until sauce has thickened. Serve hot with rice.

## Mee Goreng

**PREPARATION TIME:** 20 minutes

**COOKING TIME:** 15 minutes

**SERVES:** 4 people

8oz fine egg noodles
¼ cup peanut oil
1 onion, peeled and chopped finely
4oz pork, finely sliced
4oz shrimp, shelled and de-veined
2 cloves garlic, crushed
1 tbsp light soy sauce
1 tsp sambal manis or sambal oelek
¼ cabbage, shredded
1 green chili pepper, seeds removed,
    and sliced
2 sticks celery, sliced
Salt
Pepper

### Garnish
Sliced cucumber
Sliced green onions

Soak noodles in hot water for 8 minutes, or boil until cooked. Rinse in cold water. Drain in a colander. Set aside. Heat wok and add oil. Stir-fry onion, garlic and chili until onion starts to color. Add sambal manis or sambal oelek. Add pork, celery, cabbage and salt and pepper, and stir-fry for 3 minutes. Add soy sauce, noodles and shrimp, and toss mixture to heat through well. Place in a warm serving dish, surrounded with sliced cucumber and sprinkled with green onions on top.

## Five-Spice Beef with Broccoli

**PREPARATION TIME:** 15 minutes

**COOKING TIME:** 15 minutes

**SERVES:** 4 people

8oz sirloin or butt steak
1 clove garlic, crushed
½ tsp finely grated ginger
½ tsp five-spice powder
½ cup broccoli flowerets
Bunch of chives, cut into 1" lengths
2 tbsps peanut oil
½ tsp salt
1 tbsp dark soy sauce
½ cup hot water
2 tsps cornstarch, slaked in 1 tbsp
    cold water

Cut steak into thin slices, then into narrow strips. Mix together with garlic, ginger, and five-spice powder. Heat wok, add 15ml (1 tbsp) of oil, and stir-fry broccoli for 8 minutes. Remove broccoli and add remaining oil. Add meat, and stir-fry for 3 minutes. Add broccoli, soy sauce, salt and water, and heat to simmering point. Mix cornstarch with cold water, and pour into wok, stirring continuously until liquid thickens. Toss in chives, stir, and serve immediately with boiled rice.

**Lamb with Cherries (right), Five-Spice Beef with Broccoli (below right) and Boiled Rice (bottom right).**

# Beef with Pineapple and Peppers

**PREPARATION TIME:** 40 minutes
**COOKING TIME:** 15 minutes
**SERVES:** 4 people

1lb sirloin or butt steak, sliced thinly
1 can pineapple slices, drained and
   chopped
1 green pepper, cored, seeds removed,
   and chopped roughly
1 red pepper, cored, seeds removed,
   and chopped roughly
2 cloves garlic, crushed
1 tsp chopped ginger root

1 onion, peeled and chopped roughly
2 tbsps light soy sauce
1 tsp sugar
2 tsps cornstarch
2 tbsps water
1 tbsp peanut oil

**Sauce**
1 tbsp plum sauce
1 tbsp dark soy sauce
1 tsp sugar
1 tsp sesame oil

1 tsp cornstarch
¼ cup water
Salt
Pepper

Combine 2 tbsps of light soy sauce with 1 tsp of sugar, 2 tsps of cornstarch and 2 tbsps of water. Mix well and pour over steak. Toss together well, and put aside for at least 30 minutes, turning occasionally. Heat wok and add

peanut oil. Add ginger, garlic, onion and peppers, and stir-fry for 3 minutes. Remove from wok and set aside. Add extra oil if necessary and stir-fry beef, well separated, for 2 minutes. Remove from wok. Mix together all sauce ingredients in wok, and heat until sauce begins to thicken. Add vegetables, beef and pineapple, and toss together over a high heat until heated through. Serve with boiled rice.

**This page: Beef with Pineapple and Peppers.**

**Facing page: Duck with Orange.**

# Meals with Poultry

## Duck with Orange

**PREPARATION TIME:** 30 minutes
**COOKING TIME:** 50 minutes
**SERVES:** 4 people

1 small duck
1 tbsp butter or margarine
1 tbsp oil
3 oranges
1¼ cups light chicken stock
⅓ cup red wine
2 tbsps redcurrant jelly
1 tsp arrowroot
1 tbsp cold water
Salt
Pepper

**Garnish**
Watercress
Slivers of orange peel

Pare the rind of 2 oranges and cut into fine shreds. Blanch in hot water and set aside for garnish. Extract juice from 2 oranges. Cut peel and pith from 1 orange, and then slice into rounds, or cut flesh into sections if preferred. Wash duck and dry well with paper towels. Heat wok, and add oil and butter. When hot, add duck, and brown all over. Remove from wok and, using poultry shears or a chopper, cut duck in half lengthwise, and then cut each half into 1″ strips. Return duck to wok, and add stock, red wine, redcurrant jelly, orange juice and rind, and salt and pepper to taste. Bring to boil, reduce heat, cover and simmer gently for 20 minutes. Add orange slices, and simmer a further 10 minutes, or until duck is cooked. If sauce needs to be thickened, mix arrowroot with cold water and add to sauce. Bring to the boil, and simmer for 3 minutes. Garnish with slivers of orange peel and watercress.

## Chicken and Cashews

**PREPARATION TIME:** 15 minutes
**COOKING TIME:** 40 minutes
**SERVES:** 4 people

1 lb chicken breasts, skinned, boned, and cut into shreds

4 tsps cornstarch
1 tbsp light soy sauce
¼ cup peanut oil
2 tbsps water
1 stick celery, sliced thinly
½ cup roasted cashews
½ cup green beans, trimmed and sliced
1 clove garlic, crushed
1 onion, peeled and sliced
1 carrot, cut into matchstick strips
2 green onions, sliced

½ cup chicken stock, made from chicken bones, or ½ cup of hot water plus 1 chicken bouillon cube
½ tsp five-spice powder
Salt
Pepper

Simmer chicken bones in a little water to make chicken stock, or dissolve chicken bouillon cube in hot water. Set aside to cool. Combine half the cornstarch, the

five-spice powder, and a pinch of salt. Toss in chicken and mix well. Heat wok, add peanut oil and, when hot, add chicken pieces a few at a time, tossing well. Stir-fry until chicken just starts to change color – about 3 minutes. Lift out with a slotted spoon, and drain on paper towels. Repeat until all chicken is done. Carefully pour off all but 1 tbsp of oil. Add onion and garlic, and cook for 2 minutes. Add celery, beans, carrot, and green onions, and stir-fry for 2 minutes. Add strained chicken stock, and cook for 3 minutes until vegetables are tender but still crisp. Slake remaining cornstarch with 2 tbsps of water. Add soy sauce, and pour into wok. Adjust seasoning if necessary. Bring back to the boil and let simmer for 3 minutes. Add chicken and heat through. Remove from heat. Stir in cashews, and serve at once with noodles or rice.

## Chicken with Mango

| **PREPARATION TIME:** 5 minutes |
| **COOKING TIME:** 30 minutes |
| **SERVES:** 4 people |

4 chicken breasts, cut into shreds
2 ripe mangoes, sliced, or 1 can sliced
    mangoes, drained
4 green onions, sliced diagonally
½ tsp ground cinnamon
1 tsp grated ginger
1 tbsp light soy sauce
1 chicken bouillon cube
⅔ cup water
2 tbsps oil
2 tbsps sweet sherry
1 tsp sugar
Salt
Pepper

Heat wok and add oil. Add ginger and cinnamon, and fry for 30 seconds. Add chicken and green onions, and stir-fry for 5 minutes. Add light soy sauce, crumbled chicken bouillon cube, water and sugar, and bring to boil. Add salt and pepper to taste, and simmer for 15 minutes. Add mangoes and sherry, and simmer, uncovered, until sauce has reduced and thickened. Serve hot with boiled rice.

## Stir-Fried Chicken with Yellow Bean Paste

| **PREPARATION TIME:** 1 hour 10 minutes |
| **COOKING TIME:** 20 minutes |
| **SERVES:** 4 people |

1lb chicken breasts, sliced thinly
2 tbsps oil
2 tbsps yellow bean paste
1 tsp sugar
1 egg white, lightly beaten
1 tbsp rice vinegar
1 tbsp light soy sauce
1 tbsp cornstarch
Salt
Pepper

### Garnish

Green onion flowers (cut green onions into 2" lengths. Carefully cut into fine shreds, keeping one end intact, and then soak in cold water until curling).

Mix together lightly beaten egg-white, cornstarch, and salt and pepper. Place chicken in a bowl and pour over mixture. Toss together to coat well. Set aside in a cool place for at least 1 hour. Combine vinegar, soy sauce and sugar. Remove chicken, and set egg mixture aside. Heat wok, and add oil. When hot, stir-fry chicken until lightly browned. Remove from wok. Add bean paste to wok and stir-fry for 1 minute. Add vinegar mixture and stir in well. Return chicken to pan, and fry gently for 2 minutes. Finally, add egg mixture, and simmer until sauce thickens, stirring all the time. Garnish with green onion flowers. Serve immediately with boiled rice.

## Soy Chicken Wings

| **PREPARATION TIME:** 1 hour 10 minutes |
| **COOKING TIME:** 20 minutes |
| **SERVES:** 4 people |

2lbs chicken wings
½ tsp crushed ginger root
1 tbsp Chinese wine, or 2 tbsps dry
    sherry
1 tbsp light soy sauce
1 tbsp dark soy sauce
1 tbsp sugar
2 tbsps peanut oil
1 tsp cornstarch
2 tsps sesame oil
1 star anise
2 green onions, sliced
3 tbsps water
Salt
Pepper

Wash chicken wings, and dry on paper towels. Mix together ginger, light soy sauce, sugar, cornstarch, sesame oil, wine, and seasoning. Pour marinade over chicken wings and leave for at least 1 hour, turning occasionally. Heat peanut oil until very hot. Add green onions and chicken wings, and fry until chicken

**Chicken with Mango (left) and Stir-Fried Chicken with Yellow Bean Paste (below).**

has browned well on all sides. Add dark soy sauce, star anise and water. Bring to the boil, and simmer for 15 minutes. Remove star anise. Serve hot or cold.

## Chicken Livers with Peppers

**PREPARATION TIME:** 30 minutes

**COOKING TIME:** 15 minutes

**SERVES:** 4 people

*1lb chicken livers*
*4 Chinese mushrooms*
*1 green pepper*
*1 red pepper*
*1 tbsp rice vinegar*
*2 tsps sugar*
*1oz fresh ginger*
*1 small leek*
*3 tbsps vegetable oil*
*1 onion*

**Garnish**
*2 green onion flowers (trim and slice lengthwise, keep one end intact, and leave in cold water in refrigerator until curling)*

Soak mushrooms in hot water for 20 minutes. Clean and trim chicken livers, and blanch in boiling water for 3 minutes. Drain and slice. Peel

and finely slice ginger. Mix vinegar and sugar, and add ginger, and set aside. Clean and trim leek and cut into thin rings. Peel and slice onion and cut into strips. Core and remove seeds from peppers, and cut into strips. Drain mushrooms, remove hard stalks, and cut caps into thin slices. Heat wok, add oil,

and, when hot, add mushrooms, onion, leek and peppers, and stir-fry for 5 minutes. Remove and set aside. Add liver and ginger mixture. Stir-fry for a further 5 minutes, return vegetable mixture to wok and heat through. Serve garnished with spring onion flowers.

**This page: Chicken with Cashews (top) and Soy Chicken Wings (bottom), and Chicken Livers with Peppers (right).**

brown. Increase heat and add curry powder. Fry for 30 seconds. Add salt and vinegar, and cook for 1 minute. Add chicken, and turn so that mixture coats chicken well. Add coconut cream and milk, and simmer gently over a low heat for 20 minutes. Serve with boiled rice.

## Honey Soy Chicken Wings

**PREPARATION TIME:** 5 minutes

**COOKING TIME:** 30 minutes

**SERVES:** 4 people

1lb chicken wings
½ tsp salt
2 tbsps peanut oil
¼ cup light soy sauce
2 tbsps clear honey
1 clove garlic, crushed
1 tsp ginger, freshly grated
1 tsp sesame seeds

Heat wok, add oil, and when hot, add chicken wings and fry for 10 minutes. Pour off excess oil carefully. Add soy sauce, honey, sesame seeds, garlic, grated ginger and salt. Reduce heat, and gently simmer for 20 minutes, turning occasionally. Serve hot or cold with rice.

## Sesame Fried Chicken

**PREPARATION TIME:** 10 minutes

**COOKING TIME:** 30 minutes

**SERVES:** 4 people

1lb chicken breasts, or 4 good-sized
    pieces
¾ cup flour
1 tsp salt
1 tsp pepper
¼ cup sesame seeds
2 tsps paprika
1 egg, beaten, with 1 tbsp water
3 tbsps olive oil

Sift flour onto a sheet of wax paper and stir in salt, pepper, paprika and sesame seeds. Dip chicken breasts in egg and water mixture, then coat well in seasoned flour. Heat wok,

## Chicken Curry (Mild)

**PREPARATION TIME:** 10 minutes

**COOKING TIME:** 40 minutes

**SERVES:** 4 people

3lbs chicken
1 tbsp peanut oil

1 onion, peeled and finely chopped
2 cloves garlic, crushed
½ tsp grated ginger
2 tsps curry powder
½ tsp salt
1 tbsp vinegar
⅔ cup milk
⅔ cup coconut cream

Cut chicken into small pieces: breast-meat into 4 pieces, thigh-meat into 2 pieces, and wings separated at joints. Heat oil until hot. Reduce heat. Add onion, garlic and ginger and cook gently, stirring continuously. Cook for 10 minutes, or until onion is soft and a golden

**This page: Chili Sichuan Chicken (top) and Honey Soy Chicken Wings (bottom)**

**Facing page: Chicken Curry (Mild) (top) and Sesame Fried Chicken (bottom).**

add oil and, when hot, fry the chicken breasts until golden brown on both sides. Turn heat down, and cook gently for 10 minutes on each side. Serve hot with rice.

## Lemon Chicken

**PREPARATION TIME:** 5 minutes

**COOKING TIME:** 40 minutes

**SERVES:** 4 people

*2 lbs chicken pieces*
*⅔ cup oil*

### Lemon Sauce
*Juice of 1 lemon*
*⅓ cup water*
*2 tsps cornstarch*
*2 tbsps sweet sherry*
*Pinch of sugar, if desired*

### Garnish
*Lemon slices*

Heat wok and add oil. When hot, add chicken pieces and toss in oil until well browned. Reduce heat and cover. Simmer for 30 minutes until chicken is cooked. Remove with a slotted spoon and drain on paper towels. Place chicken pieces in a serving dish and keep warm. Meanwhile, carefully drain oil from wok. Slake cornstarch in 2 tbsps of water. Put lemon juice and remaining water in wok, and bring to the boil. Add cornstarch, and stir until boiling. Simmer for 2 minutes until thickened. Add sherry and sugar, and simmer a further 2 minutes. Pour over chicken pieces and garnish with lemon slices. Serve with boiled rice.

## Chili Sichuan Chicken

**PREPARATION TIME:** 40 minutes

**COOKING TIME:** 20 minutes

**SERVES:** 4 people

*4 chicken breasts, sliced thinly*
*1 clove garlic, crushed*
*1 green pepper, cored, seeds removed, and diced*
*1 red pepper, cored, seeds removed, and diced*
*1 red chili pepper, seeds removed, and sliced finely*
*1 green chili pepper, seeds removed, and sliced finely*
*1 tsp chili sauce*
*1 tbsp light soy sauce*
*1 tsp Chinese wine, or dry sherry*
*½ tsp cornstarch*
*Salt*
*Pepper*
*¾ cup peanut oil, for deep frying*

### Sauce
*1¼ cups chicken stock*
*2 tsps cornstarch*
*1 tsp Chinese wine, or dry sherry*

Mix together 1 tsp wine, ½ tsp cornstarch, light soy sauce, and a pinch of salt and pepper. Pour over chicken and mix well. Leave to marinate for at least 30 minutes. Heat oil for deep frying in wok. When hot, toss in sliced chicken and fry until just coloring and cooked through. Drain well. Carefully remove all but 1 tbsp of oil from wok. Heat, and when hot, add garlic, green and red peppers, green and red chili peppers, and chili sauce. Fry gently for 2 minutes. Stir 2 tbsps of chicken stock into cornstarch, then pour remaining chicken stock and wine into wok. Add cornstarch mixture and stir well, until sauce boils and thickens. Add chicken, and toss until heated through. Serve with rice.

## Chicken Cacciatore

**PREPARATION TIME:** 15 minutes

**COOKING TIME:** 30 minutes

**SERVES:** 4 people

*1 lb chicken breasts, cut into bite-sized pieces*
*1 16oz can plum tomatoes*
*1 onion, peeled and sliced*
*1 green pepper, cored, seeds removed, and sliced*
*½ cup mushrooms, sliced*
*2 cloves garlic, crushed*
*1 tsp basil*
*1 tsp oregano*
*1 bay leaf*
*2 tsps tomato paste*
*½ cup dry white wine*
*3 tbsps olive oil*
*Salt*
*Pepper*

### Garnish
*Parsley*

Heat wok and add 1 tbsp oil. When hot, add chicken and stir-fry until chicken is opaque – about 8 minutes. Add more oil if necessary. Remove with slotted spoon and set aside. Heat remaining oil, and add basil, oregano and bay leaf, and fry for 1 minute. Add onion and garlic and stir-fry until onion is soft but not colored. Add green pepper and mushrooms, and fry for a further 3 minutes. Add undrained tomatoes, tomato paste, wine, and salt and pepper to taste. Cook uncovered for 10 minutes. Return chicken to pan, and stir until heated through. Garnish with parsley and serve with spaghetti.

Chicken Cacciatore (left) and Lemon
Chicken (below).

# Vegetables, Chutney and Sauces

## Sweet and Sour Cabbage

**PREPARATION TIME:** 5 minutes

**COOKING TIME:** 20 minutes

**SERVES:** 4 people as a vegetable

*Half a small cabbage*
*2 tbsps butter or margarine*
*3 tbsps vinegar*
*2 tbsps sugar*
*3 tbsps water*
*Salt*
*Pepper*

Slice cabbage into shreds. Melt butter in wok. Put cabbage into wok with other ingredients and set over a moderate heat. Stir until hot, then cover and simmer for 15 minutes. Adjust seasoning if necessary. Serve hot.

## Gado Gado

**PREPARATION TIME:** 20 minutes

**COOKING TIME:** 30 minutes

**SERVES:** 4 people as a vegetable

*1 cup bean-sprouts*
*1 cup Chinese cabbage, shredded*
*½ cup green beans, trimmed*
*Half a cucumber, cut into 2" strips*
*1 carrot, peeled and cut into thin*
*    strips*
*1 potato, peeled and cut into thin*
*    strips*
*1 tbsp peanut oil*

**Peanut Sauce**
*2 tbsps peanut oil*
*⅔ cup raw shelled peanuts*
*2 red chili peppers, seeds removed,*
*    and chopped finely, or 1 tsp chili*
*    powder*
*2 shallots, peeled and chopped finely*
*1 clove garlic, crushed*
*1 tsp brown sugar*
*Juice of half a lemon*
*¼ cup coconut milk*
*⅔ cup water*
*Salt*

**Garnish**
*Sliced hard-boiled eggs*
*Sliced cucumber*

Heat wok and add 1 tbsp peanut

oil. When hot, toss in carrot and potato. Stir-fry for 2 minutes and add green beans and cabbage. Cook for a further 3 minutes. Add bean-sprouts and cucumber, and stir-fry for 2 minutes. Place in a serving dish. Make peanut sauce. Heat

wok, add 2 tbsps peanut oil, and fry peanuts for 2-3 minutes. Remove and drain on paper towels. Blend or pound chili peppers, shallots and garlic to a smooth paste. Grind or blend peanuts to a powder. Heat oil and fry chili paste for 2 minutes.

**This page: Gado Gado with Peanut Sauce.**

**Facing page: Stir-Fried Vegetable Medley (top) and Sweet and Sour Cabbage (bottom).**

sugar in wok. Bring to boil, and simmer, uncovered, for 10 minutes. Add mango and raisins, and simmer gently until sauce is thick. Serve cool as an accompaniment to a curry.

**Left: Sweet-and-Sour Sauce (top), Mango Sauce (center) and Chili Sauce (bottom). Tomato Chutney (right) and Mango Chutney (bottom).**

Add water, and bring to the boil. Add peanuts, brown sugar, lemon juice, and salt to taste. Stir until sauce is thick – about 10 minutes – and add coconut milk. Garnish vegetable dish with slices of hard-boiled egg, and cucumber and serve with peanut sauce.

## Sweet and Sour Sauce

**PREPARATION TIME:** 10 minutes

**COOKING TIME:** 10 minutes

*Juice of 2 oranges*
*2 tbsps lemon juice*
*2 tbsps white wine vinegar*
*1 tbsp sugar*
*1 tbsp tomato paste*
*1 tbsp light soy sauce*
*½ tsp salt*
*1 tbsp cornstarch*
*2 tbsps water*
*Drop of red food coloring if desired*

Combine orange and lemon juice, sugar, vinegar, tomato paste, soy sauce, salt, and red coloring (if desired). Place in wok and heat gently. Blend cornstarch with water, and stir into sauce. Bring to boil and simmer for 3 minutes, stirring continuously. Good with fish, pork, wontons and spring rolls (egg rolls).

## Mango Chutney

**PREPARATION TIME:** 5 minutes

**COOKING TIME:** 20 minutes

*1 can mango slices, drained and*
*    chopped*
*1 cup white wine vinegar*
*2 cloves garlic, crushed*
*1 tsp chopped ginger root*
*½ tsp five-spice powder*
*1 tsp salt*
*¼ cup sugar*
*2 tbsps golden raisins*
*Pinch chili powder (optional)*

Place vinegar, salt, garlic, ginger, five-spice powder, chili powder and

## Ginger Sauce

**PREPARATION TIME:** 5 minutes

**COOKING TIME:** 10 minutes

1 tbsp grated ginger root
2 tbsps light soy sauce
1 tbsp Chinese wine, or dry sherry
1 tsp sugar
1 tsp cornstarch
2 tbsps water
1 tbsp oil

Heat wok, add oil and gently fry ginger. Mix together soy sauce, wine and sugar. Blend cornstarch with water, and add to soy/wine mixture. Pour into wok and bring to the boil. Simmer for 3 minutes, stirring continuously. Push through strainer. Good with sea-food, pork, beef and crab rolls.

## Brinjal Bhartha

**PREPARATION TIME:** 20 minutes

**COOKING TIME:** 30 minutes

**SERVES:** 4 people as a vegetable

2 large eggplants, cut into 1" slices
3 tbsps oil
⅔ cup water
1 onion, peeled and chopped finely
2 green chili peppers, seeds removed, and sliced very thinly
½ tsp ground cumin
Pinch of sugar
2 tsps lemon juice
Salt

Slice eggplants and sprinkle with salt. Set aside for 15 minutes. Rinse off salt and dry with paper towels. Heat wok and add 2 tbsps of oil. Fry eggplants in hot oil, browning lightly on both sides. When all oil has been absorbed, add water. Cover and simmer for 15 minutes, or until eggplants are soft. Remove from wok, and drain. Heat remaining oil in wok. Add onion, ground cumin and chili peppers, and cook gently for 5 minutes without coloring onion. Meanwhile skin eggplants, and push flesh through a strainer or blend. Add onion mixture to eggplants. Add sugar, lemon juice and salt to taste.

## Special Fried Rice

**PREPARATION TIME:** 15 minutes

**COOKING TIME:** 20 minutes

**SERVES:** 4 people

2 cups boiled rice

4oz shrimp, shelled and de-veined
8oz Chinese barbecued pork, or cooked ham, diced or cut into small pieces
1 cup bean-sprouts
½ cup frozen peas
2 green onions, sliced diagonally
1 tbsp light soy sauce
1 tsp dark soy sauce
2 tbsps peanut oil
Salt
Pepper
**Pancake**
2 eggs, beaten

Salt

### Garnish
2 green onion flowers (trim green onions, slice lengthwise, leaving one end intact and leave in cold water in refrigerator until curling).

Heat wok and add 1 tbsp of peanut oil. Roll oil around surface. Make pancake by mixing beaten eggs with a pinch of salt and 1 tsp of oil. Add egg mixture to wok, and move wok back and forth so that the mixture

spreads over the surface. When lightly browned on the underside, turn over and cook on other side. Set aside to cool. Heat remaining oil in wok. When hot, add green

**This page: Special Fried Rice (top) and Ginger Sauce (bottom).**

**Facing page: Brinjal Bhartha (top) and Okra and Tomatoes (bottom).**

onions and peas and cook, covered, for 2 minutes. With a slotted spoon, remove and set aside. Re-heat oil and add rice. Stir continuously over a low heat until rice is heated through. Add soy sauces and mix well. Add peas, green onions, bean-sprouts, meat, shrimp, and salt and pepper to taste. Mix thoroughly. Serve hot, garnished with pancake and green onion flowers. The pancake may be sliced very finely and mixed in if desired.

## Julienne of Vegetables

**PREPARATION TIME:** 20 minutes

**COOKING TIME:** 15 minutes

**SERVES:** 4 people as a vegetable

2 medium onions, peeled and cut into matchstick strips
2 carrots, scraped and cut into matchstick strips
1 parsnip, scraped and cut into matchstick strips
2 sticks celery, cut into matchstick strips
1 turnip, peeled and cut into matchstick strips
1 tbsp oil
2 tbsps water
1 tbsp butter
Salt
Pepper

Prepare vegetables. Heat wok and add oil. Stir-fry vegetable strips over gentle heat for 5 minutes. Add water and salt to taste, and increase heat. Cook for a further 5 minutes over high heat. Drain any liquid from wok. Add butter and freshly-ground black pepper, and toss to coat well.

## Mango Sauce

**PREPARATION TIME:** 5 minutes

**COOKING TIME:** 20 minutes

1 can sliced mangoes
2/3 cup malt vinegar
1/2 tsp garam masala
1 tsp grated ginger root
1 tbsp sugar
1 tsp oil
Salt

Heat wok and add oil. Add garam masala and ginger, and cook for 1 minute. Add undrained mangoes, vinegar and sugar, and salt to taste. Simmer, uncovered, for 15 minutes. Blend and push through a strainer. Good with chicken, beef and spring rolls (egg rolls).

## Stir-Fried Vegetable Medley

**PREPARATION TIME:** 20 minutes

**COOKING TIME:** 10 minutes

**SERVES:** 4 people as a vegetable

2 carrots, cut into flowers (slice strips out lengthwise to produce flowers when cut across into rounds)
1 can baby corn, drained
2 cups broccoli flowerets (slit stems to ensure quick cooking)
1 onion, peeled and sliced in julienne strips
2 sticks celery, with tough strings removed, sliced diagonally in half-moon shapes
1 zucchini, sliced diagonally
1 clove garlic, crushed
1 tbsp light soy sauce
1/4 tsp finely-grated ginger
2 tbsps oil
Salt
Pepper

Prepare all ingredients before starting to cook. Heat wok and add oil. Add ginger, garlic, onion, carrots, broccoli and zucchini, and toss in oil for 2-3 minutes. Add celery and baby corn, and toss 1-2 minutes longer. Season with soy sauce, and salt and pepper if desired. Add cornstarch to thicken vegetable juices if necessary.

## Ratatouille

**PREPARATION TIME:** 30 minutes

**COOKING TIME:** 30 minutes

**SERVES:** 4 people as a vegetable

1 eggplant, sliced into 1" slices
2 zucchini, sliced diagonally
4 tomatoes, chopped roughly
2 onions, peeled and quartered
1 red pepper, cored, seeds removed, and chopped roughly
1 green pepper, cored, seeds removed, and chopped roughly
3 cloves garlic, crushed
1 tsp dry basil
1/4 cup olive oil
Salt
Pepper

Slice eggplant and sprinkle with salt. Leave for 20 minutes. Rinse in water, and dry on paper towels. Chop roughly. Heat wok and add oil. Add onions, garlic and basil. Cover and cook gently until onion is soft but not colored. Add peppers, zucchini and eggplant. Cover and fry gently for 15 minutes stirring occasionally. Add tomatoes and salt and pepper to taste and cook covered for a further 10 minutes. Serve hot or chilled.

## Tomato Chutney

**PREPARATION TIME:** 5 minutes

**COOKING TIME:** 15 minutes

4-6 ripe tomatoes, chopped roughly
1 cup white wine vinegar
1/2 tsp garam masala
1 tsp salt
2 tbsps sugar
2 green chili peppers, seeds removed, and chopped finely
1 tsp chopped root ginger
Pinch chili powder (optional)

Place tomatoes, vinegar, salt, garam masala, chili powder, chili peppers, sugar and ginger in wok. Bring to boil, and simmer, uncovered, for 15 minutes or until thickened. Serve cool as an accompaniment to a curry.

## Okra and Tomatoes

**PREPARATION TIME:** 15 minutes

**COOKING TIME:** 10 minutes

**SERVES:** 4 people as a vegetable

8oz okra, sliced into 1/2" pieces
1 onion, peeled and chopped
2 tomatoes, chopped
1 red chili pepper, seeds removed, and sliced finely
1/4 tsp turmeric
1/4 tsp chili powder
1/2 tsp garam masala
1 tbsp oil or ghee
2/3 cup water
Salt

Heat wok and add oil or ghee. When hot, add turmeric, chili powder and garam masala, and fry for 30 seconds. Add onion, okra and red chili pepper, and stir-fry for 3 minutes. Add tomatoes, water, and salt to taste, and cook uncovered for 5 minutes or until sauce thickens.

## Chili Sauce

**PREPARATION TIME:** 5 minutes

**COOKING TIME:** 10 minutes

4 tbsps tomato paste
1/2 tsp chili powder
2 tbsps Chinese wine, or dry sherry
2 tbsps white wine vinegar
2/3 cup water
1 tsp cornstarch
2 cloves garlic, crushed
1 tsp grated ginger root
1 tbsp dark soy sauce
1 tbsp sesame oil

Heat wok and add oil. When hot,

**Ratatouille (right) and Julienne of Vegetables (bottom right).**

add garlic and ginger and fry for 1 minute. Mix together tomato paste, chili powder, wine, soy sauce and vinegar. Add to wok. Blend cornstarch with 1 tbsp of water and add to wok with remaining water. Bring to the boil and simmer for 3 minutes, stirring continuously. Good with sea-food, beef, vegetables and spring rolls (egg rolls).

# Sweets

## Bananas Cooked in Coconut Milk

**PREPARATION TIME:** 20 minutes

**COOKING TIME:** 20 minutes

**SERVES:** 4 people

4-6 large, ripe bananas, peeled and
  sliced diagonally into 3 or 4 pieces
1 tbsp brown sugar
1 cup desiccated coconut
⅔ cup milk

### Garnish
*Desiccated coconut*

Put sugar, coconut and milk into
wok, and bring to simmering point.
Turn off heat and allow to cool for
15 minutes. Push through strainer
or a piece of cheesecloth to squeeze
out juices. Return to wok, and
simmer for 10 minutes, or until
creamy. Add bananas, and cook
slowly until bananas are soft. Serve
immediately sprinkled with
desiccated coconut.

## Steamed Custard

**PREPARATION TIME:** 10 minutes

**COOKING TIME:** 20 minutes

1⅓ cups milk
2 tbsps sugar
2 eggs, beaten
½ tsp vanilla extract
Sprinkling of ground nutmeg or
  cinnamon

Place sugar and milk in wok. Heat
gently until the milk reaches a low
simmer and the sugar has dissolved.
Remove from wok and leave to
cool for 5 minutes. Meanwhile,
wash wok and place steaming rack
inside, with 1½"-2" of hot water.
Return to heat and bring water to
simmering point. Pour milk and
sugar mixture over beaten eggs.
Beat again, and add the vanilla
extract, stirring well. Pour mixture
into a heat-proof dish or metal
molds and sprinkle lightly with
nutmeg or cinnamon. Place on rack
and cover with waxed paper, so
condensation does not drop into
custard. Cover wok and steam for
10-15 minutes. To test if cooked, a
knife inserted in center will come
out clean, and custard will be set
and gelatinous. Cover and cool for
1 hour, then place in refrigerator
until needed.

## Bananas Flambés

**PREPARATION TIME:** 5 minutes

**COOKING TIME:** 10 minutes

**SERVES:** 4 people

4 firm, ripe bananas, peeled and cut
  in half lengthwise
¼ cup unsalted butter
¼ cup brown sugar
3 tbsps brandy
Juice of 2 oranges

Heat wok, and add half the butter.
When hot, add bananas, rounded
edge down, and fry until golden on
underside. Add remaining butter,
and carefully turn the bananas over,
so their flat sides are in contact with
the wok surface. Sprinkle with
sugar, 1 tbsp of brandy, and orange
juice, and allow to simmer for
3 minutes. Heat remaining brandy,
set alight, and pour over bananas.
When flame is extinguished, serve
immediately. (Flaming can be done
in serving dish).

## Sesame Toffee Apples

**PREPARATION TIME:** 45 minutes

**COOKING TIME:** 30 minutes

**SERVES:** 4 people

2 large, firm Granny Smith or
  Golden Delicious apples
1 tbsp flour

### Batter
2 tbsps flour
2 tbsps cornstarch
1 large egg
2 tbsps water
1 tsp sesame oil

Oil for deep frying
⅓ cup peanut oil
2 tsps sesame oil
½ cup sugar
2 tbsps white sesame seeds

Peel, core and cut apples into 1"
chunks. Toss in 1 tbsp of flour.
Combine flour, cornstarch, egg and
sesame oil in a small bowl. Mix to a
batter with water and leave for
½ hour. Place oil for deep frying in
wok, and heat to a moderate
temperature (350°F; 180°C). Put
fruit in batter and coat well. Deep
fry several pieces at a time until
they are golden. Remove with
slotted spoon and drain on kitchen
paper. Repeat until all fruit is fried.
Repeat process to fry fruit a second
time for a couple of minutes.
Remove with slotted spoon and
drain. When fat has cooled,
carefully drain and clean wok. Fill a
bowl with cold water and ice cubes,
and put on side. Put peanut and
sesame oil and sugar into wok, and
heat until sugar melts. When it
begins to caramelize stir and add
sesame seeds and then add all of
fruit. Toss around gently to coat in
caramel. Take out quickly, and drop
into iced water a few at a time, to
prevent sticking together. Serve at
once. (This can also be made with
sliced bananas).

Facing page: Bananas
Flambés (top) and Sesame
Toffee Apples (bottom).
Steamed Custard (right) and
Bananas Cooked in Coconut
Milk (below).

# Glossary

**Arrowroot.** The starchy extract of the ground root of an American plant, used as a thickening agent for sauces.

**Bamboo Shoots** (family: *Gramineae*). A native of Asia, this is the spear-shaped core of the young bamboo plant. The more tender winter variety is preferable, and can be purchased pre-cooked and canned in water. It should be drained before use, and will keep well in a dish in the refrigerator for up to 10 days if covered with fresh water that is changed daily.

**Bean Curd.** This fresh, white, custard-like curd cake, high in protein and hence very nutritious, is made from ground soya beans and gypsum. It is also available dried, fried, and in a yellow variety which contains less water.

**Bean Paste.** There are many varieties of this soy bean based paste. Hot, with the addition of chili peppers, is hot and salty. Sweet, with the addition of garlic, tomato paste and spices, is hoi sin sauce. Yellow, made with crushed yellow soy beans, is salty.

**Bean Sprouts** (Bean Shoots). These are the young, crisp sprouts of the green mung bean, and sometimes the soy bean. Available canned and fresh, the latter being preferable, and will keep for 2-3 days if covered with plastic wrap and kept in a cool place. They are inexpensive, and can also be grown successfully at home.

**Black Beans,** fermented. Used in sauce-making, these whole beans are fermented and preserved in salt and ginger, and then dried and sold in plastic bags, or canned in brine. To remove excess saltiness, they should be soaked in cold water for about 10 minutes. Drained, and then crushed and used, they impart a pungent flavor to the dish. Black bean sauce can be purchased ready-made.

**Chili Peppers.** There are numerous varieties of chili peppers varying in size and strength of flavor. Commonly used in Eastern cooking are the red and green finger-like chili peppers, about 4″ long, and the tiny red and green birds'-eye chili peppers which are very hot. When preparing chili peppers, it is advisable to wear rubber gloves and avoid getting the oils near lips or eyes. The seeds, which are very hot, should be discarded unless a fiery dish is desired.

**Chili Powder.** Dried fruit-pod of the capsicum plant in flaked or powdered form. It is very hot and spicy, and should be purchased only in small quantities.

**Chinese Rice Wine.** A strong wine made from glutinous rice. A good substitute is dry sherry if it is unobtainable.

**Chives** *Allium schoenoprasum.* Now available in most parts of the world, they have a subtle onion taste and bright green stems which are used, snipped, as a garnish for soup and other dishes.

**Cinnamon** *Cinnamomum zeylanicum.* Delicate, sweet spice which is the dried, aromatic bark of a type of laurel. Sri Lanka and the Seychelles both produce this spice, which can be purchased in bark, quill or powder form.

**Clarified Butter** – Ghee. This is ordinary butter cleared of its impurities. When ordinary butter is heated, the top surface is skimmed clean, and when the sediment constituting milk solids has settled to the bottom, the golden liquid that is poured off is now clarified. With a higher burning point than most other oils, it is ideal for stir-frying and sautéing. It is also ideal for sealing pâtés.

**Cloves** *Eugenia aromatica.* The dried, aromatic buds of a type of myrtle native to South East Asia. Used whole, or with the central bud ground into a powder. A spice with preserving properties, it is used in sweet and savory dishes.

**Coconut Milk.** Liquid extracted from white flesh of coconut. Can be made with desiccated coconut by adding hot water or hot milk, the latter being creamier, and letting stand until cool, with coconut milk squeezed out and the pulp discarded. Canned coconut milk can be purchased, but is expensive.

**Coriander** *Coriandrum sativum.* Chinese parsley. The fresh leaves and seeds of this plant are used, and are available in most parts of the world. The leaves have a fresh, pungent flavor, and are often used to garnish fish and chicken dishes. The crushed seeds in powder form are an important ingredient in curries.

**Cornstarch.** A fine, white maize flour used as a thickener, mainly for sauces.

**Cumin** *Cuminum cyminum.* The pungent, hot and rather bitter-tasting dried fruit of a plant related to parsley. This spice is very popular, and is an important ingredient in curries. It can be used whole or ground, and is an essential ingredient in garam masala.

**Curry** *Chalcas koeniggi.* The leaves of this South West Asian plant are used fresh or dried, and are a basic curry ingredient.

**Curry Powder.** Generally found only in the West, it is a blend of different spices, which combination can vary from mild to hot.

**Dried Mushrooms** *Lentinus edodes*. Shiitake. Tree fungus found in the East on oak logs and shii trees. They are sold dried, and have to be reconstituted by soaking in hot water for about 20 minutes. Drain, cut away stems and discard, and slice or dice cap. They are expensive, but only a few are needed to impart their distinctive woody flavor to a dish.

**Five-Spice Powder.** The combination of ground star anise, Sichuan pepper, fennel seeds, cloves and cinnamon. This fragrant mixture is often used to marinate soy-braised or roasted meat or poultry.

**Garam Masala.** A mixture of ground, roasted spices, usually consisting of coriander, cinnamon, cumin, cloves, dill, fennel, ginger and pepper. A flavoring used in many Indian dishes, it can be bought ready-made.

**Ghee.** See Clarified Butter.

**Ginger** *Zingiber officinale*. The root-stem of this South East Asian plant can be purchased whole, sliced, or ground. The whole root can be peeled as needed, and used sliced, chopped or grated. It freezes well and can be used without thawing first.

**Julienne Strips.** Cut into equal matchstick strips. Size can vary according to length of cooking time.

**Noodles:** Egg, Rice, Cellophane. *Egg:* require little preparation at home as they are usually pre-cooked by steaming. *Rice:* common in Southern China and, as their name suggests, are made from rice. *Cellophane* – transparent: usually made from mung bean starch paste, and used often in soups.

**Nutmeg** *Myristica fragans*. The dried kernel of a type of myrtle. It can be purchased whole or ground, and is used in powdered form.

**Oils:** Sesame, Peanut. *Sesame:* oil extracted from the seeds of the sesame plant. *Peanut* – groundnut: oil extracted from groundnuts.

**Oregano** *Origanum vulgare*. Available world-wide, its leaves are usually used dried.

**Oyster Sauce.** Thick, brown sauce made from extract of oysters, and sold bottled. Often used in Chinese cooking, its rich, subtle taste lends to other ingredients, whether meat, vegetables, noodles or rice. Can be added to a sauce, or used as a dip.

**Paprika** *Capsicum tetragonum*. A type of dried pepper, paprika varies from mildly hot to mild and sweet, and rosy-brown to scarlet in appearance.

**Rice:** Basmati, Patna, White Glutinous. *Basmati:* narrow, long-grain rice; one of the finest and most expensive. Grown in the Himalayan foothills, it has a subtle flavor, and is firm and separate when cooked. Best to eat with Indian food. *Patna:* long-grain. This versatile rice is very popular and is grown world-wide. The grains are hulled and polished, and when cooked remain firm, fluffy and separate. Good to eat with Chinese food. *White Glutinous:* very popular in Chinese cooking, particularly in sweet dishes.

**Rice Paper.** A wafer made with paste of flour, salt and water and cooked between hot irons.

**Rice Vinegar.** Made from rice, this is a clear, mild vinegar. A good substitute is white wine vinegar.

**Saffron** *Crocus sativus*. The dried stigmas of the Autumnal Crocus, this aromatic spice imparts a slightly bitter flavor and a bright yellow coloring to food, especially rice, and is one of the world's most expensive spices.

**Sambal Manis.** A combination of chili peppers and spices, often used as an accompaniment to Indonesian food, or in cooking, is mild and slightly sweet.

**Sambal Oelek.** A combination of chili peppers and salt, used in cooking – particularly Indonesian dishes.

**Slake.** Mix with a small quantity of liquid before adding to a liquid for thickening.

**Soy Sauce.** Used extensively in Chinese cooking, this sauce is made from soy beans. There are two types: dark soy sauce is thicker and not as salty as light soy sauce and gives a brown hue to food; light soy sauce is thinner and saltier than dark soy sauce, and used often in cooking.

**Star Anise** *Illicium verum*. The dried fruit of an evergreen tree native to China. This is an 8-pointed, star-shaped, reddish-brown spice. It can be purchased in powder form or whole. It has a strong aniseed flavor and smell, and is used to flavor stewed and braised meat and poultry dishes. It is also one of the spices that go into five-spice powder.

**Turmeric** *Curcuma Longa*. The dried and ground root stems of one of the ginger family. A vivid yellow powder, it is a spice often used in curries.

**Water Chestnuts.** These nuts are sweet and crisp, and are sold pre-peeled and canned in water.

**Wonton Wrappers** – Skins. Very thin wrappers made from a mixture of wheat, egg and water. They are sold fresh, usually in 3″ squares, and freeze well.

**Worcestershire Sauce.** A hot sauce containing malt vinegar, molasses, chili peppers, spices and tropical fruits. It is used sparingly.

# Index